"From the landing of the first pilgrims on the eastern shore of the New World to the most recent selfless acts of service here and abroad, stories make up the tapestry of American exceptionalism. In this compelling book by Dr. George, natural-born and immigrant citizens of the greatest nation on Earth show by way of their experiences how the Bible, the Declaration of Independence, and our Constitution birthed a country unparalleled in human history. Read it, and then read it with your family. The dividends will benefit your legacy for generations to come."

— LtGen. William "Jerry" Boykin, USA (Ret.), served 36 years in the Army, is now EVP of the Family Research Council and the best-selling author of *Never Surrender*

"My work on 'The Hill' has recently changed from being a US senator to becoming president of the Heritage Foundation. What hasn't changed is my passionate desire to see America pulled from the brink of the socialist abyss and back to its first principles. One of our strategies in this pursuit is to tell the unvarnished truth about the American experience. The stories you are about to read in this book exemplify what is noblest and best about this grand experiment in republican government. A government formed on the basis of the preeminence of God and the equality of all people, people who reach for their best when freedom and the rule of law are maintained. This book is a must-read for every man, woman, and child."

— Jim DeMint, president of the Heritage Foundation and author of *Saving Freedom*

"*My Story of America* reminds us of the true greatness of our nation. Today, more than ever before, we must be reunited with that Divine Hand of Providence that lead the first settlers to this land and sustained following generations through numerous trials and tribulations. Through this inspiring book, Dr. Michael George brings to life the experience of individuals seeking the freedom of life, liberty, and the pursuit of happiness in America."

— Barry Loudermilk, Georgia State Senator, author of the book *And Then They Prayed*

My Story
of America

My Story
of America

*Inspirational Stories of Life, Liberty,
and the Pursuit of Happiness*

MICHAEL T. GEORGE

Freedom Congress Books
Portland, Oregon

Cover design: Kyle Cannon
Author's photo: copyright © Xandria Maurer
Interior design: Lisa Parnell, lparnell.com

ISBN: 978-0-9896750-0-0 (paperback edition)

This book is dedicated to

my son,

whose character and integrity inspire me every day.
The countless hours traveling, writing this book,
and telling the story of America is all done so that
hopefully you will be able to grow up
in a country that still values faith and freedom.
Always remember that I love you.

Contents

Foreword
by LtCol Oliver L. North

On the eve of Operation Iraqi Freedom, the command-ing general of the 1st Marine Division distributed a one-page "Message to All Hands." It was a succinct warning to those going into battle about what to expect from the enemy and the general's expectations for the Marines. His instructions and encouragement on deport-ment, skill, courage, and compassion harkened back to Shakespeare's rendition of *Henry V* on St. Crispin's Day and Eisenhower's guidance to his troops going ashore at Normandy. The close, an admonition paraphrasing Ro-man general Lucius Sulla: "Demonstrate to the world there is 'No better friend, no worse enemy' than a US Marine," is now an axiom in the Marine Corps.

Some members of the media who read the letter ex-pressed amazement that a Marine division commander—about to go into combat—could be so eloquent. Those of us who have known Jim Mattis a very long time weren't surprised at all.

When we first met four decades ago, James N. Mattis was a brand-new second lieutenant, a bright, enthusiastic student, and I was a tactics instructor at The Basic School (TBS) in Quantico, Virginia—where newly minted Marine officers are introduced to what it means to be an officer of Marines. He had a mischievous glint in his eye, a half-suppressed smile, and a can-do spirit matching his physical fitness. Though nick-named "Mad Dog" for his speed and agility on the O-Course, he was also a voracious reader. It's my recollection he was one of the few who completed the lengthy TBS "professional reading list" that began at Sun Tzu, waded through Clausewitz, and ended with Vietnam.

While he was a student in 1973, then-Lt. Mattis and Capt. North "co-starred" in a Marine recruiting film shot while his class was going through training. His is one of the very few student names audible in the grainy rendition available on YouTube.

The following year, after we served in 3rd Division, he told comrades I had given him a "fail" in platoon tactics. In 2004, he repeated this story after his "jump command group" repelled an attack on Route Michigan in Anbar Province. Not so. Lt. Mattis did have a "do-over" on a live fire range when I stopped training because the weather made it unsafe to pro-ceed—but "Mad Dog" Mattis never failed at anything in his long service as a US Marine.

His command experience at every rank is extraordinary, even by Marine standards. As a second lieutenant, Mattis led a rifle platoon and weapons platoon in 3rd Division. While a captain, he commanded a rifle company and weapons company in 1st Marine Brigade. As a major, he commanded a recruiting station. As a lieutenant colonel, he commanded 1st Battalion, 7th Marines in Operation Desert Storm. And as a colonel, he commanded the entire 7th Marine Regiment.

In each of these assignments he honed his leadership skills and unsurpassed tactical proficiency. His subordinates recollect how he inspired them by never asking others to do something he wouldn't have done. Those who served with him at Amphibious Warfare School, Marine Corps Command and Staff College, and National Defense University claim he was already known as the "Warrior Monk" when they met him the first time.

By the time our paths crossed again in 2001, America was at war and Brigadier General Jim Mattis was commanding Task Force 58—a Marine Expeditionary Brigade—and I was reporting for *Fox News*. TF 58, the first conventional US combat unit deployed to Afghanistan, was en route to Forward Operating Base Rhino in Kandahar Province. Had it not been for Jim Mattis, I would never have been allowed to go ashore.

In March 2003, Griff Jenkins, my *Fox News* cameraman/field producer, and I were with Major General Jim Mattis and his 1st Marine Division as they closed in on Saddam Hussein's capital. Though we couldn't broadcast it then, we heard him order his Marines to "Go heavy kinetic all the way to Baghdad." They did.

Blunt-spoken "Mattis-isms" are now part of Marine lexicon, folklore, and mythology. Some are even tattooed on Marine biceps. But I've also heard Jim Mattis in quiet moments of reflection. In 2004, shortly before he relinquished command of the 1st Marine Division, he sat down with our camera rolling at the 2nd Battalion, 4th Marines command post in Ramadi,

Iraq. I asked him what he wanted our people at home to know about his Marines.

He paused and replied, "We proved to the world that we have young Americans with a level of selflessness . . . willing to put up with danger and discomfort and protect this experiment we call the United States of America. This experiment will continue so long as we have young people willing to mix it up in a fight. The enemy has learned the hard way, don't mess with us."

Jim Mattis and his radio call sign, "Chaos," are now retired. He will miss keeping company with heroes. I'll miss seeing my friend Jim Mattis in a flak jacket and helmet.

What makes America great is its people. During my years reporting for *Fox News*, it has been my privilege to have our nation's best as my "beat." What you've just read exemplifies the nature and character of the men and women who faithfully serve in our military.

You are about to read a valuable collection of other real life stories that combine to paint the colorful and even majestic portrait of America, the greatest nation on the face of the Earth. We hope you are inspired by these stories to preserve and defend our Constitution from all enemies, foreign and domestic.

Semper Fi—
LtCol Oliver L. North, USMC (Ret.)

Oliver North is a nationally syndicated columnist, the host of War Stories *on the Fox News Channel, and author of the* New York Times *bestseller* Heroes Proved *from Threshold Books. He's also the co-founder of Freedom Alliance, an organization that provides college scholarships to the children of US military personnel killed or permanently disabled in the line of duty.*

Acknowledgments

My deep appreciation goes out to my family and friends; without their help I would have never been able to finish writing this book. I am truly thankful for your love and support. Never be afraid to stand for what is right, for in so doing you keep alive the spirit of Liberty.

O SAY, *Can You* See?

S tanding in front of my truck, an unfamiliar sound traveled through the air. The sixth sense I developed from war immediately took over as my instincts dropped me to the ground. Debris flew past my body as the roof on the building behind was ripped asunder. I felt the wind of a disabled airplane as its propeller narrowly avoided removing my head. Death had repeatedly knocked on my door, but I refused to answer. Once again I cheated him out of his prize.

My name is Errol. This is my story of America.

What a man experiences in his life will mold him into the person he will ultimately become. How he chooses to deal with those experiences will result in either a positive or negative view of life. My life is no different, and as I sit here recalling the highs and lows, I cannot help but think how one event shaped my life in an amazing way. The event to which I refer occurred in Vietnam, but the story begins in America.

I grew up in a small town where seven of us lived in a house the size of a single-car garage, across the street from a canning factory. My mother and father, two brothers, two sisters, and me were all crammed into this box we called home. Upon entering through the front door, you arrived in the kitchen and a small bedroom was to the right. From the kitchen you went through a little door into the living room, and off to the left was a small bathroom we all shared.

I know you must be thinking, *Where did all these people sleep?* Well, it was a challenge. My dad took part of the living room to build a very small bedroom. That is where he and my mom slept. My brothers and I slept in the little bedroom room off the kitchen in bunk beds. My sisters got the short end of the deal and had to sleep in what was left of the living room. It may sound like a difficult arrangement, but we knew nothing else in life so it just seemed normal to us.

Sharing a room with two older brothers was not always fun; in fact, for James and me, it was downright miserable at times. Our oldest brother Richard's favorite pastime was to beat us up. Now I am not talking about little boyhood skirmishes; I mean physical assault. He literally pounded on us until we could not take it any longer. Bruises, black eyes, and bloody noses were only a few of the remnants of his assaults. I don't ever remember where my parents were when this was happening; I just know they were not around. James and I most certainly wanted this behavior to stop, but we had no clue how to make that happen, so we just endured it.

Saturday morning rolled around like it did every week, and Richard decided he would spend the whole day making our lives miserable. For the entire morning and into the afternoon we experienced horrific beatings from him. At one point he stopped for just a moment. He turned to us and said, "I am going to the bathroom, and when I come back you are going to get it some more." I am sure you can understand the fear we both faced. At that time I was seven years old, and James was ten. We both looked at each other and agreed something must be done.

Above the mantel in the living room was my father's single-shot, twelve-gauge shotgun. We had been instructed never to touch it, but in this scenario James and I decided it would be our savior. Quickly we went into the kitchen and returned with a chair. James stepped up on the seat and grabbed the weapon from the posts. It was loaded and ready for action. We positioned ourselves directly to the left of the bathroom door. I raised the gun as James aimed the barrel, then we waited for Richard. Seconds seemed like hours to me as I held the gun in place. As the door to the bathroom slowly opened, I nervously held the weapon tightly. Richard came out, stepped around the corner, and POW! James pulled the trigger. The shot hit Richard in the legs, almost taking them both off. Screams of terror raced from his voice as he lay on the ground bleeding. James fell backward from the recoil of the blast, and my hand burned from the barrel. We were dazed, Richard was bleeding, but we knew then he would never hurt us again.

Richard lived through the incident, and the police swept the whole thing under the rug as an accident. I don't think James and I really knew how bad we could hurt him; we only knew we wanted him to stop before he killed one of us. We wanted to be free from his tyranny. This same desire for free-dom would be a yearning in my soul throughout my life, but finding it would prove difficult.

As you can already see, I grew up in an interesting household. My brother, James, and I were close growing up, but as he got older he became a stone-drunk alcoholic. In fact, it is the way he died. One night at his kitchen table he was drunk and died of a massive heart attack. James spent his life in and out of prison. Robbery, rape, arson, and murder were only a few of the sins that put him behind bars. Some men never find peace, and James seemingly never did.

Richard was a street rider. I know you are probably won-dering, *What is a street rider?* Well, a street rider is a per-son who takes parts from old cars and makes street rods, cars people race on the streets of a city. He had a shop where he built parts for cars manufactured before 1948, and people ev-erywhere in the city came to him to fix their hot rods. He had FBI agents, congressmen, and a governor come into his shop looking for just the right piece to make their car a classic. I learned from my brother that people who race street rods are a closed group. When Richard introduced me to them, he just said this is a friend of mine and never told me their names; I only knew their occupations.

Richard had the knowledge and connections to be quite a wealthy man, but he was too much of a thief for that to ever materialize. Given the opportunity, he would steal the gold fill-ings out of your teeth. He had little integrity and no morality; in fact, an entire wall in his living room was filled from floor to ceiling with porno movies. Here was a man with the skill and talent to do anything he wanted, yet he died a crook and a pervert. Even through all the trouble and heartache I experienced with him, I still loved him very much. He died much like James, without peace.

As a boy, I spent most of my time with my brothers, but I did enjoy being around my two sisters. My oldest sister died in 2012, and to the end, she too seemed to be searching for some elusive something. I don't even remember how many men she married and divorced in her lifetime, but at the age of eighty she was still searching for the right man who would complete her life. My younger sister was married with a couple of kids but left her family in the 1960s and moved in with another woman and remains there to this day.

Yet, no matter what transpired in my life, I had a deep sense of love and compassion for my siblings. The same can be said about my parents. My father was an atheist who worked in a research laboratory and believed anything spiritual was phony, just a bunch of fairy tales.

Now my mother was an interesting figure; she suffered terribly from asthma and the most I ever saw her weigh was ninety-eight pounds. She was a habitual smoker, addicted to Camels and Lucky Strikes. Anytime she heard the commercial for Lucky Strikes during a radio program she gave me a quarter and sent me to the store for a package of cigarettes. My, how times have changed!

My mother grew up on the Flathead Indian Reservation, and she was quite the spiritualist. She practiced the black arts, meaning she followed the daily horoscopes religiously and offered her fortune-telling services to anyone who desired. Having a fortune-teller mother is a little strange for a young boy, and I admit at times it made me feel quite uneasy. Were these the only things she dabbled in, I might have been OK; but there was another, much more disturbing activity. My mother conducted séances; she actively consulted the dead for guidance and words from beyond. There is something very eerie about the whole practice, and it always made me feel very uncomfortable.

If this was not strange enough, my mother also carried a bag of chicken bones with her and she rolled those bones out on the floor and read them to see what was going to happen. I never understood what she saw and how she read them, but on more than one occasion she was right. I can remember one morning my mother got up and rolled the chicken bones out on the table. She looked at them for quite a long time, studying them over and over. She then went to get the keys to the car and told me to come with her. We drove for a little while until we arrived at a graveyard. As we got out of the car, she pointed to a statue of Jesus standing in the middle of the cemetery. She looked at me and said, "Next week I will be buried at the left hand of that statue." I was frozen in silence. What she said fell over me like a lead blanket, and I did not know what to think. We got back into the car, and on the drive home I pondered what my mother said. I saw some silly and crazy things with my mother, but this seemed to take the cake.

During the next few days, I did not think much about what occurred, but the early part of the week came around and my mother suddenly collapsed with a heart attack. Quickly we did what we could, and my father got her to the hospital. When we arrived they immediately took her in and began to do everything medically possible to save her life. Moments later the doctor came out to give us the news.

They told us that over the years smoking and asthma had weakened her heart muscles. There was nothing they could do, and my mother died shortly thereafter. I still remember the pain and loneliness I felt when we were told my mother died. However that painful loneliness took an eerie turn days later.

On the day of the burial I stood in the street near the same cemetery my mother and I visited days earlier. I now watched them bury her body to the left of the statue of Jesus. It happened just like she said; did the chicken bones tell her what was going to happen or was it something greater? It would be a question I pondered for quite some time.

Thinking again about my mother dying reminds me of the times I cheated death as a child. I can recall numerous instances.

In one particular occasion, I was home recuperating from a tonsillectomy. As I was lying in my bed, I began having a seizure and started swallowing my tongue. All air to my lungs was completely shut off.

My mother happened to look over into the bedroom where she saw me turning blue. She was panicked but still able to think clearly. Immediately she ran to the kitchen to get a wooden spoon. She rushed back into my room and wedged the spoon into my mouth. She did everything she could to fish my tongue from the back of my throat. She was successful, and I began breathing again.

She saved my life.

I remember another time when I was a small boy I was out playing in the yard. Totally oblivious to my surroundings,

I wandered into the street. Suddenly I heard a car, and when I turned I saw it sliding toward me, trying to stop.

I was paralyzed with fear, my heart beating faster every second. I stood there as it careened at me while the panicked driver tried to get the vehicle under control.

Miraculously the car stopped sideways in the road with the door pressed against my pant legs. Mr. Death came up empty again. Events like these made me wonder if there was someone or something greater looking out for me.

After my mother's death, I began to drift in life and my well-being definitely became a concern as I started attending a new high school in California. It did not take me long to start getting into major trouble.

The school was dominated and run by two gangs, and I certainly did not help my situation by drinking alcohol regularly. I drank a half-pint of liquor on my way to school then a full pint on the way home. As a teenager, I was consuming a fifth of liquor every day. As a boy without a mother and with a father uninterested in me, I was a powder keg with just a few inches of burning fuse left.

One day, I decided to take an eight-foot bullwhip with me to school. I sewed it into the inner part of my jacket. As I got into my truck I checked to make sure the pistol I carried in my seat was still there. I had no intention of starting trouble, but I was definitely going to be ready if it came looking for me.

I got to school and headed to my homeroom just like normal. Each morning we were to stand and say the Pledge of Allegiance to the stars and stripes. Even though I was a rough troublemaker, I knew the importance of being an American. I was very patriotic and knew freedom did not come cheap.

That morning as we stood to say the pledge, several kids decided they were going to protest and not stand to honor our country. I am not sure what went through me as I walked over to the corner and picked up a baseball bat, but I was enraged at the disrespect being shown. I gripped the bat tight as I swung and hit the first kid. I almost tore the top of his head off. Another guy turned and threatened me, so I took out the bullwhip from the lining of my coat and began to rip the clothes and skin off him. Needless to say, but I will, I was now in big trouble and got to spend some quality time with the local authorities.

What occurred next is really just a blur, but I do remember standing before a very kind judge in Oakland who looked me square in the eye and asked me, "Son, are you going to graduate?" I told him, "No sir, probably not." So he said, "I highly recommend you go into the military. Either you are going to go, and they are going to teach you something, or I am going to say a few words and someone else is going to teach you something. What do you want to do?" So I went and told my dad I was headed to the military. It certainly seemed like the better of the two options.

So I was off to the military. They sent me to Fort Polk in Louisiana for basic training, and once I was finished I transferred to Fort Leonardwood in Missouri where I was placed with combat engineers. After I was there for a while I decided I wanted to go to jump school, so they sent me to Fort Benning, Georgia, and upon graduation I was made a member of the 82nd Airborne.

I was not with the unit for very long before they gave me some gear and put me on a flight to the Dominican Republic.

We were deploying to the region to prevent Cuba from trying to take over Santa Domingo. Fidel Castro and his Communist cronies had their eyes on the land of some free people, and we went to stop him. We really never saw much combat; we simply looked for a few rebels and drove up and down a lot of hills and in and out of some jungle areas.

One day while out on patrol, we were in our jeep heading up the side of a hill. What we didn't know was rebels had dug a jeep trap across the road on the other side of the hill. There was no way we were able to see it in time.

Our jeep had a large anti-personnel, anti-tank weapon on the back. As we headed down the hill, we hit the trap, causing us to flip. It all happened so fast, but it seemed like the sky was now below my feet and death was staring me in the face. When we finally quit rolling, the anti-tank gun was between the jeep, the ground, and me. The gun kept the jeep from crushing me to death. I was sore but still alive. Some of the other guys were not so fortunate. I started to think I was a cat with nine lives.

After this brief bit of excitement I returned to the states. I was home for only a few days when a good friend of mine contacted me. He was newly married and was excited for me to meet his new wife from Georgia. So we made arrangements for a hunting trip and headed south. I did not realize at the time, but his wife had a sister and I was being set up for a blind date. I always like to tell people I went to Georgia to hunt quail and came back with a two-legged dear. Yes, I married that girl.

We were not married for very long when I got orders to head to Vietnam. Getting ready to go overseas required me to go through several schools, such as jungle warfare, to get prepared for the mission. Upon completion I was deployed to Southeast Asia. I was with a combat gun unit at the time, and

I stayed with them for about six months up through the battle of Hue City.

We lost a lot of good men during this time; the attrition rate was very high. Because there was a lot of combat wounded, I decided to extend my tour and transfer into a Special Operations Group unit. I was with them for about six months, and because of the great loss of life we experienced, our unit was disbanded, so I was granted a short leave and came back to the states.

I was excited to return, but I was not ready for what I was about to experience when I got home. I heard all kinds of stories about how unpopular the war was and the protests happening on college campuses. I flew into California, and the plane landed at Travis Air Force Base. After arrival they put me on a bus headed for downtown Oakland then dropped me off near Kaiser Hospital, which was just down the street from the University of California at Berkeley campus. Traffic was congested due to the construction going on nearby.

The hot California sun seemed stifling as I stood there in full military attire with black bag in hand waiting for the next bus to take me to my home. I was not there very long until a crowd began to gather.

Two dudes wearing sandals approached me with looks of cockiness written all over their faces. Within minutes one of them started really railing on me. "Hey baby-killer. Are you proud of all the children you have slaughtered? You know you are nothing but a lousy piece of crap."

I stood there as he called me every foul name under the sun, and not one person in the crowd said anything; they just waited and watched. I decided I could stand and take it as long as none of them touched me. Arrogantly the guy to my left came over and spit in my face.

Slowly I turned and lowered my black bag. That's when I noticed a piece of 2x4 about a couple feet long. When I sat my bag down I came back up with the piece of lumber and hit the guy as hard as I could right in the mouth. He just kind of spun around and fell over. The other guy took off running in utter fear. The coward had called me every name in the book, but now he wanted no part of me. I chased him about a block until he stumbled on one of his sandals. Dazed and confused he turned to look back to see where I was. To his dismay I was right behind him and closing fast. As he got up to run I swung away, and the force of my blow sent him flying through the air like a home run by Babe Ruth. He just rolled down the street when he hit the ground. He had nothing more to say.

Immediately, I felt two big hands under my right arm and another set under my left, and the only things I could see were badges. All I could do was shake my head as the police led me back to their car where they placed me in the back seat.

Reluctantly I asked if they could please get my black bag I left on the street down near the bus stop. So they both got in the car and pulled up to the area where I left my bag. The dude I hit with the 2x4 was still lying face down. They walked over, got my bag, and got back into the car, then we headed toward downtown Oakland. They never said anything to the guy lay-ing on the ground; they just looked at him.

One of the officers turned, looked at me, and asked, "So, when did you get back?" I told him, "Just now." He smiled and said, "I cannot believe they let you out where they did. We were sitting across the street the entire time watching the events take place. We knew it was probably not going to turn out well. Anyway, where are you going?" I began to feel at ease so I told him where home was, and they asked me if I had eaten and I told them, "No."

Before I knew it, they were buying my lunch at the Doggie Diner and driving me almost all the way home. In fact, they radioed another patrol car to meet them, and those officers drove me the rest of the way to my house. The whole time I thought I was headed to jail; instead, these guys wanted to thank me for my service. I still remember them to this day, and I am sure those sandal-wearing dudes from Berkeley still remember me as well.

I was not home for very long when I was called back to Vietnam to work with the Military Assistance Command. They assigned me to the 14th Arvin Regiment, and I became a part of the small special ops group (SOG). Most of the people who made up this unit were Cambodians and Montagnard, or Mountain Yards as we called them. One of the officers told me each one of these men was worth ten of the enemy. At first I thought they must be joking, but after I saw the way they handled themselves in a firefight I came to realize it was true.

I always met interesting and dynamic people while I was in Vietnam, and Lloyd W. Pate was certainly one of those individuals. He was held captive for thirty-two months by the Communist Chinese during the Korean War and survived long periods of starvation, dysentery, solitary confinement, and a five-hundred-mile death march in the freezing cold. The subhuman conditions Pate endured rendered him a man without any emotions or feelings whatsoever—none, zero!

In my entire life I was never around a man like this; sometimes it amazed me and sometimes it scared me to death. This numbed man became my partner; Pate and I were unit leaders in the same SOG team. I learned a lot of good things from Lloyd W. Pate; however, I was also learning to dull my sensibilities. This would not be a good thing.

Words cannot express the level of depravity that occurs during war. It is a terrible thing to go to war, but it is a worse thing to lose your freedom. The South Vietnamese wanted to keep their freedom, and the Communist North Vietnamese wanted to take it from them. Patrick Henry once said, "Is life so dear, or peace so sweet, as to be purchased at the price of chains and slavery?" What is the use of living if you can't have freedom? We were willing to die to help them keep their liberty.

Every day brought a new battle, whether it was one in the jungles or one in my mind. Unfortunately I was slowly becoming more like Lloyd Pate. To illustrate the point, I remember on one occasion standing in a rice patty full of leaches. I was just involved in a firefight with the Vietcong; I was exhausted and hungry.

I looked to see if there was anywhere I could sit down and have lunch; all I saw was leach infested rice patties. So I improvised; I took several dead North Vietnamese and stacked them into a pyramid then climbed on top of them to eat my lunch. There was no emotion; I just did not want to sit in the water and fight off leaches while I ate.

This was my condition, and something dramatic needed to take place or I knew I would lose myself in a black hole.

Help for my condition came days later when I was walking back to my little grass hut. The monsoons had arrived, and the rain was coming down in sheets. It was all I could do to see a foot in front of me. Any shelter would be a welcomed sight so when I noticed a bombed out building, I decided to check it out. I knew I would have to be careful because areas like these were good places for the enemy to hole up.

As I walked in I saw nothing of any interest—no weapons, no ammunition, and no enemy—but something in the corner caught my eye. The rain was pouring through an opening in the roof as I made my way over to the object. I reached down and picked up a Gideon's New Testament. I was not sure at the time why I felt it was important, but I knew I was compelled to take it with me. So I placed it in my pocket and later headed back to my grass hut.

When I returned, I pulled the little book from my pocket. We were right in the middle of the monsoon season and the rains soaked everything. Inside the hut I had an airbed with a mosquito net draped over the top. I climbed onto my bed and took out a small penlight and began to read. We had a German Shepherd dog someone over there gave us, and he scooted up next to me as I read. For the most part he was a great companion.

The story began to captivate me, and I read it for quite some time until I could barely keep my eyes open. I placed the book beside my bed and turned off my light. As I turned over, my eyes were drawn to some green beady little eyes staring back at me. Cautiously I turned to Lieutenant Prater and told him to shine his light above my net because something was staring at me. He began to laugh as he turned his light my way. That is when I saw the biggest spider I have ever seen. He was hanging just above my face inside of my mosquito net. The only thing I knew now was I wanted out from under the net, but there was one problem; I was stuck. The dog was lying on the corner of the net beside my bed, and the more I pulled to try to free myself, the closer the spider got to my face.

After some careful negotiation I managed to get out just as the net collapsed onto my bed. Prater was laughing hard at me as I ran over to get my .45 pistol. When I got back to my bed, I noticed the spider was trapped upside down under my mosquito net, its legs kicking in all directions. I aimed my weapon and pulled the trigger three times—no more spider and no more airbed.

Prater looked at me with a huge smile and said, "So how is your bed?" Needless to say I was not happy, and the dog never moved throughout the entire incident. He just looked at me like I was stupid; in this case he was right.

Reading that little New Testament was the only smart thing I did that night. I read it from the beginning all the way to Psalms 28 or Palms 28 as I called it then. I did not totally understand everything I was reading, but it did seem to bring peace in the midst of my trouble. If there was anyone who needed peace in the midst of trouble, certainly I did. As an American I knew I was free, but as a person, I had no peace and felt like a slave inside.

A few days later, I arose with an uneasy feeling of foreboding. I felt today was going to be a very bad day. In fact one of the other guys looked at me and said, "You look like today is going to be a bad day." I don't know how he knew, but it must have been written all over my face.

Well, come 1:15 p.m. my worst feelings became reality. The sun was beating down as three of us made our way through an area of rice patties. The Mountain Yard guide carrying my radio in front of us accidently triggered a big land mine. The explosion was enormous. Dirt, metal, and blood filled the sky as everything became black in front of me. When I regained consciousness I realized I was blown some thirty feet from the mine. I was on my knees in water to my chest with my M-16 rifle above my head. I looked down and thought, *Man, I was not here a moment ago. I wonder what happened.*

> *God who gave us life gave us liberty.*
> — THOMAS JEFFERSON

As I looked over to my left, I saw our guide was blown into several pieces and the bottom part of the radio had big holes in it. The lieutenant on my left was thrown quite some distance away, but I could see him lying face down with several chunks missing from him. As I began to stand I noticed something drastically wrong. I was hit in my left side. As I looked down I could see my internal organs. With a sick feeling coming over me, I took off my shirt and tied it around my waist to keep my guts from falling out. I stumbled over to the guide, taking the radio from what was left of his hand. Within seconds I put on a new antenna so I could radio for help. The only helicopter I could reach was a transport, but he agreed to try to fly in to get us.

The wait seemed like forever, but within minutes he was there. We managed to get the lieutenant loaded into the chopper and what was left of the Mountain Yard, then I was helped aboard. They took us to the MASH hospital just outside Can Tho, Vietnam. I do not know to this day if the lieutenant lived or died, but he was in bad shape.

When we arrived I was immediately taken into surgery. Everything was so hectic, and because of the absolute chaos surrounding the situation, the doctor performing the surgery accidently sewed a surgical sponge inside me. That mistake would almost kill me. It was a good thing I had not used all nine of my lives yet.

It is often said men in war are willing to die for one another because of the brotherly love and bond that grows between them. This is so true, and the guys with me were just as great. While I was in the hospital they went to my grass hut and brought some things to me they thought I might want; one of the items was that Gideon's New Testament. I shipped it home to the states so it would not be lost. I figured it must be important because I found it and it now found me.

Because of the fragile nature of the MASH hospital I was only there for about a week, then they shipped me to Japan for more treatment under safer circumstances. By the time I arrived in Japan, I was not doing well. My fever was through the roof and a staph infection set in. They decided they had better x-ray me to see if they could determine the cause of my problems. Moments later a doctor came rushing up to me with x-ray in hand and began to show me everything in it. He first pointed out scrap metal, some other garbage, and then he focused my attention on one round image. He said, "Errol, what you are seeing is a surgical sponge. All surgical sponges have a metallic band in them so they will show up on x-ray. So you my friend are headed back to surgery so we can remove this sponge and stop the fever and staph infection threatening your life."

After surgery I was hooked up to a machine. I'm not quite sure what they called it, but every three hours they woke me and pumped warm saline solution into my stomach. They continued to do this until I could safely be moved. They then put me aboard a nightingale flight to Alaska.

I must say if ever there was any group cheated out of praise and appreciation it would have to be the staff aboard the nightingale flights from Vietnam. The plane was loaded with wounded soldiers, and the doctors and nurses worked wonders in the air. I was in the middle of the plane, and the guy on the bed below me had one arm and both legs missing.

Listening to the moans and smelling the stench of death, my mind took me back to an event that occurred in Hue City. In the middle of combat, a helicopter operator came on the radio saying, "We are hit and we are going down; tell my wife and kids that I love them." I can still remember the words and his voice to this day, but what really cuts through me was his demeanor. He was not crying; he was not upset; he was perfectly calm. The manliness of his voice froze me in my tracks. The man had great peace; his words and his voice reassured me as I lay there on my back being transported through the skies to Alaska.

As we started to make our descent into the airport and the cabin began to depressurize, the blood pressure in the man below me began to drop. The medical staff worked feverishly to save him. One of the doctors turned and said, "Well, we are probably going to have to leave him in Alaska so that he can survive." Immediately the man began to cry out, "Don't take me off this plane; I would rather die on my way home then be left here. Please don't take me off this plane!" He sobbed and cried through his pleadings.

Now every wounded man on that plane who could talk started saying, "Leave him on the plane, if he wants to die on the way home, let him die on the way home. Just leave him on the plane." Of course they did not listen to us, and I often wonder what ever happened to that young man.

After a brief stop in Alaska we were flown to Washington, and I was transported down to Martin Army Hospital at Fort Benning, Georgia, near my home. I was there for some time and was starting to progress a bit. I was at least able to get up and move around so I called it progress.

The doctor came on a Saturday and asked me where I lived. I told him about fifty miles south. He turned and said, "I am going to let you out on convalescence leave. I want you back in the hospital one week from Monday." My wife and brother-in-law were there, and they agreed to have me back on the appointed date.

It felt good to be in the states, and my wife and her family took me down to the local Wal-Mart and bought me some clothes. They purchased a large shirt so I wouldn't have to tuck it in my pants. The bandages wrapped around me made many things difficult. Then on the next day I did something I had never done before in my life; I went to church.

They took me to a little cinderblock church in a small town near the edge of a cornfield. The church was so small; when you sat on the back row you could literally reach over with one hand and grab the door exiting the church. That's where I chose to sit. I knew if I got sick or had complications I would need to leave quickly. Neither did I know what to expect, so I wanted to be able to make a hasty retreat if necessary.

The pastor was an interesting fellow; he was bi-vocational. He was a meat cutter by day and a preacher on the weekend. When he stood he let his message fly with all he had. He preached hell hot and heaven glorious. I had never heard anything like it in my life, and as soon as he finished we left.

I really did not know what to think about the whole thing, but come Wednesday I decided to pray; this was the first time I ever prayed in my life. I still remember what I prayed, "Lord, if you will let me live until next Sunday, I will do whatever it takes to get right with you."

When I was in Martin Hospital I thought about all the things I read in the New Testament I found in Vietnam, and two things came to my mind: What happened to the lives of all those men who died in Vietnam; I mean, where did the life go? And if this New Testament were to be true, I was in trouble or at least I felt I was at the time. This is what I was experiencing during the week I was out on convalescence leave. My life was about to be reshaped in a way I could never imagine.

Sunday came and no one in my wife's family, including my wife, was going to church. My wife and mother-in-law were both sick, the goldfish died, and the bird was lying dead in the cage. Every reason not to go was there, but I knew I had to go; I needed to go. In fact I wanted to go; it was the first time in my life I wanted to go to church and no one was going. Then I heard my brother-in-law beating on the side of the house trailer where we were staying, and he asked, "Do you want to go to church?" I answered in the affirmative, and he came in and helped me get dressed.

After dressing, he took me out to the car and attempted to put me in his Volkswagen Karmann Ghia, which is like a roller skate with a hood on it; it was that small. I looked at him and asked, "How do you expect a man my size, with staples and stitches to hold his guts in, to get in this little two seat automobile?" He said I could ride on the hood. I thought better of it, so I got on my knees, turned backward, and eased into the car.

After all the turmoil we finally arrived at the church, and he got me out of the car and into the building. I found my place on the back row with my hand near the door, and I waited for the wild man everyone called pastor.

To me he preached the exact same message he did the week before because it had the same effect on my soul. I knew I needed what he offered, and I knew I had to keep the promise I made to God on Wednesday. The service was about over, and everyone was standing, singing what they called the invitation song. I could not tell you what song they sang; I just noticed in the book they were holding it had only four verses, and we were on number three.

Sometime during the service a young woman stepped into the church and asked me to scoot over so she could sit on the end of the row. She was now in between me and where I needed to go. I turned to the girl and said, "Pardon me." She looked at me, confused, and said, "What?" I could not take it any longer. I just elbowed her out of the way, and she tumbled into the aisle. I stepped out and headed to the front. My brother-in-law thought I was mad and was going to cause trouble, so he just kept his head down.

The preacher was a little uneasy when he looked at me and asked, "Can I help you?" I told him yes and began to explain to him all I was going through. The man took his Bible, opened it, and showed me a few verses; and moments later I found peace and freedom—True Freedom!

When a man finds peace, something changes on the inside, but the results don't always show immediately on the outside. Even when you do show a change, others are quick to doubt because they knew who you were before. So for years my wife and some of her family were waiting for me to return to my former ways.

See, I was always a man who disappeared on Friday night and stayed drunk until Monday. I drank liquor and chased women all weekend long, and that was the man they knew most of their lives. They just really did not understand what truly occurred in my life. I was transformed; I was redeemed.

Anyway, once I got out of the hospital, my wife and I headed to Fort Bragg where I would be stationed until I was transferred to a teaching post at the Citadel. During this time we were attending a small church, and I began to be convicted about the idea of becoming a preacher. Now before you stop reading and decide to go and do something else, you must realize I thought I found freedom and in a sense I truly did. However, later in life I met some people who totally redefined the word, and it is through my journey of becoming a preacher we were introduced.

I was no stranger to confrontation—you have already clearly seen that—and I certainly was not spared it because I was going down the path of becoming a minister for God. I remember one occasion before I began teaching at the Citadel. An old sergeant whose name was Sova was a rough individual and meaner than a snake. He parachuted with the 503rd in the Second World War into Salerno, Italy, and he would fight at the drop of a hat.

We were both in a group known as the IRF (Initial Ready Force), and they locked us in for a month. In other words we could go nowhere; we were on standby to be sent anywhere in the world in a moment's notice.

One day we were all sitting around when Sova turned to me and said, "Hey Bible-thumper, what is wrong with my boy?"

Forty-three men sat around awaiting my answer, but they were not prepared for what I was about to say.

"Sova, the only thing wrong with your boy is you! Who gets drunk and spends all his money at the NCO club? You do. Who gets drunk and drives down the road ricocheting his car off the other cars in the street? You do. Who is it, when he can't find his house key, drives his car through the front door of his home? You do. Who goes in drunk and tears up all the furniture in the house? You do. Who passes out in the front yard and almost freezes to death? You do. So Sova, the only thing wrong with your boy is you."

You could have heard a feather hit the floor; every person in that room was expecting to see one hell of a fight. I just sat there and looked at him as he looked back. He never said a word; he just went over to the other side of the room and sat down. I was told later Sova started going to church. I don't know if it was true, but for his boy's sake I hope it was.

I know people in the room that day thought I was probably going to be killed, or at least severely beaten, but like I told you before, I seemed to be a cat with nine lives. I began to feel as though God had a specific purpose for my life or He was sparing me for some reason. That truth grew exponentially one night when my wife and I pulled into the parking lot of our church.

It was a special night of services, and we were having a dinner beforehand. I parked the truck at the side of the building beside a small pine tree. I got out and headed around to the other side of the truck where my wife handed me some food through the window.

My wife and baby girl were still sitting in the passenger side of the truck when the airplane I mentioned earlier crashed into the church. It sounded like a bomb had gone off. Shards of metal flew everywhere as the tip of the wing scrapped across the windshield of our truck leaving behind a brightly colored mark. It stopped after hitting a few cars and a house. I quickly got to my wife and daughter and held them as I realized once again my life had been spared.

Life was changing so fast, and shortly thereafter I received orders to head to Germany to help form a combat support company. While I was in Germany I met a man doing a lot of work behind the Iron Curtain. These were the countries of Poland, Hungary, East Germany, Bulgaria, Czechoslovakia, and Romania. The Communist Regime of the Soviet Union controlled them. This man was working hard to keep alive the ideals of freedom and the virtues of liberty, but more importantly he was determined to take to them the changing power of the gospel of Jesus Christ. After a short time spent with this man, I understood the importance of his mission. I developed a hunger to help take faith and freedom to these people, so when I returned home I went to Bible College in preparation for ministry and an upcoming life as a missionary behind the Iron Curtain.

I was so captivated by the devotion of the few people I had already met in those Communist countries. Their devotion to the Lord seemed to be much greater than anything I experienced with anyone else. Elderly people would walk for miles in the snow then stand in the woods to hear someone read and preach from the Bible. The things they would do to just have a copy of Scripture was amazing. One group made a printing machine out of an old washing machine and bicycle parts, and they used it beneath a pigpen outside Kiev. They went down into this little room and sealed off everything to print more copies of the Bible. Their commitment was amazing, and it was life changing for me.

So when the time came, my wife and I made the move to Germany and decided we would dedicate ourselves to taking freedom behind the Iron Curtain. Our friends at home were firmly behind us, and American churches provided us support in this effort.

While in West Germany we lived two separate lives. One life was lived out in the open, and one was secret. I built my own cars and remodeled old ones so I could put secret compartments in them. We did anything we could to smuggle items to the persecuted believers. The more I worked with these people I began to notice something interesting. The Communists may have been able to take away their freedom, but they could not take away their peace.

If you were a Christian in those Communist countries, you were denied all medical treatment, and you were only allowed to be educated as far as grade school. They allowed you to hold no job other than one of a common laborer, and often they would come and take your children away from you. On one occasion the Communists came into the home of a man who was a preacher. They looked at him and said, "We told you if you did not quit this preaching, we would take your children away from you." I turned and watched as the man spoke to his six- and eight-year-old boys. "Sons, you know we have talked about this a lot; are you prepared?" With tears running down their cheeks, they turned and said, "Yes Daddy." The man hugged and kissed his boys and watched as the Communists took them. I felt completely devastated, and the parents were broken but remarkably calm and filled with peace.

Two weeks later the Communists brought those boys back to their home. They rather hatefully looked at the man and said, "You have already ruined these boys; we can do nothing with them." Angrily they left, slamming the door behind them. The whole story came out later. The boys were taken to an orphanage where they were treated very badly, but instead of cowering in fear the boys began to sing songs about Christ and tell all the kids about their wonderful God of the Bible. No matter what the Communists did to them, it did not deter these youngsters. They were determined to share the good news in the orphanage. So because the kids would not quit, they decided to bring them back home before they "corrupted" the others.

It was amazing to me to see young people with the courage to stand for truth in a land of lies and darkness. I watched one afternoon as a group known as the "Light to the East" was interviewing a ten-year-old boy. They asked, "Son, where is your daddy?" He turned to them and said, "He is in prison for preaching the Bible." I choked back tears as the questioning continued. "So what do you want to do when you grow up?" With a firm resolve on his face, the boy proudly said, "I want to be a preacher just like my daddy."

The man stopped a moment and then said, "Don't you realize that if you become a preacher you will go to prison just like your daddy?" The boy stood up just as straight as he could and rubbed his hand across the rags he wore. Then with tears running down his face, he said, "Sir, I know that the heroes of the boys that live in the Western world are great big men who play with little rubber balls, but my hero is Moses standing at the Red Sea telling the children of Israel to stand still and see the salvation of the Lord. My hero is Joshua at Jericho and Paul on Mars Hill. But sir, the greatest hero of them all is my daddy."

I walked out of that little shack of a house and into the weeds out back and cried like a baby. I thought to myself, *If there is anything America needs, it is for daddies to become heroes to their children again.*

I can share with you story after story of people fighting for the freedom to openly practice their faith. Their stories will inspire you and make you weep at the same time—stories of people who have great peace but no freedom. I can also share stories of many men who fought in Vietnam but are still trapped. They have no peace even though they have freedom.

I have shared with you my story because America is right now still a place where you have the freedom to practice your faith; we need to treasure this gift and fight for it. I guess I can sum up everything with just a few brief words I heard from a little old man trapped behind the Iron Curtain. He said, "In Christ I am free. The Communists might be able to keep me in, but they will never be able to keep me down." He made me realize where there is no faith, there truly is no freedom. True freedom comes through faith, but that is not surprising because the apostle John stated, "If the Son sets you free, you will be free indeed!"

I understand now why the Pilgrims risked everything to come to America; they wanted to settle in a land where they would have the freedom to apply their faith. They discovered that where there is faith and where there is freedom you then can have

liberty!

BY THE
Dawn's
Early Light

Two uniformed officers were standing at the end of the street in front of us. Frightened, we turned to go the other way and encountered two more making hast toward us. Grabbing our two children, we ran toward the small dilapidated building. My fists throbbed as I pounded on the door pleading, "Please open up. I am a citizen!" Our only path to safety now slowly opened as I forced my way inside. The cries from my family filled the air as the officers grabbed at their legs. With super-human-like strength I pulled them into the dwelling and slammed the door. We were now safe inside the embassy, but for how long?

My name is Harald. This is my story of America.

★ ★ ★

I was born in 1954 in the country of Germany—a normal, healthy baby boy. Because of the Second World War, Germany at this time was a country divided into four occupied zones. The French, British, and American zones were unified into the country known as West Germany. The Russian occupational army had the other zone because they could not get a united Germany under their control; they decided to form the country of East Germany.

Everything in East Germany was controlled by a central government. They called the new nation the German Democratic Republic, but it was neither democratic nor a republic; it was whole-heartedly communist. East Germany was a pure dictatorship through and through. This occurred around 1949, five years before I was born.

Until the formation of East Germany, you could freely cross from one zone into the other; all you needed was an identification card. However, after the formation of East Germany, the Russians insisted on making the border watertight. Fences were built, streets were blocked, and barbed wire was strung. The German people had just come through the savage rule of Adolph Hitler and his political party of National Socialism; now they would experience the total control of Communism.

Around June 17, 1953, the workers in East Germany started a political uproar. They were tired of the relentless number of hours they were being forced to work by the new government. Communism brought harder, longer hours for much less pay so they decided to revolt. Over the next four days East Germany became a slaughterhouse with more than forty thousand people killed. The Russians came into Berlin with tanks and artillery, killing more than nine thousand people in the city.

The East German resistance at this time hoped the Americans would come rescue them, but because of the risk of nuclear warfare with Russia, the Cold War began and a stalemate ensued. The world sat back and watched as the Communist machine destroyed the East German people.

The city of Berlin would now be the only place you could cross the border from East into West Germany. Every East German who could flee did so at this time. For every one person who stayed, there were one thousand people who left East Germany. My family made a move also; however, we chose to move in the other direction—from West Germany into East Germany. Why would we want to do such a thing? Why would my mother with her seven children move into this land of totalitarian control? It is because she was a Communist, and at the tender age of two, I would become one also.

I grew up in a small village about two hundred miles from Berlin. We lived there until I was about thirteen, then we moved to the top of East Germany near the Baltic Sea where my mother's sister lived. This was my home for my formative years, and when I turned fourteen I pledged my allegiance to the Communist Worker Party. You had no choice; this was what you had to do at the age of fourteen. However, I was instructed in the centrally controlled government education system, and I wanted to be a Communist. They had total control over our education; we were not encouraged to learn anything from home. "Educational instruction is best left with those who are qualified and know how to educate children." This was the unwritten slogan of our Communist education department.

I was never encouraged to learn any biblical knowledge of any kind, whether it be from the school system or from my mother. However, my grandmother did insist we go to confirmation. It was her way to counteract the pledge we made to the Communist party. There was a German pastor who came to our village in an attempt to educate us about the Bible, Jesus, and the Lutheran church. He had pictures of West German soccer players, which were like sports trading cards to us. He talked with us about God, and I tried to barter with him for those cards.

The Communists did not like Bible preachers, and they did whatever they could to get them to leave East Germany. Some of the kids were greatly influenced by the pastor, but the propaganda of the teachers resulted in turning most children into good little Communists and Marxists. Unfortunately, I listened well in school, which resulted in my being a strong Communist by the time I graduated. I bought into every piece of propaganda these Stalinists pushed through the school system.

Because my schooling was now complete, I had to do an eighteen-month enlistment in the East German army. You could refuse to serve with a weapon if you were able to prove you had a Christian background all of your conscience life and had a relationship with the church. If this were the case, they would allow you to be a construction soldier, but you would be required to spend twenty-four months in the army instead of eighteen.

A construction soldier did not carry a gun. They basically were used to improve borderline security by building walls and security fences. The Lutheran and Catholic churches in West Germany heavily protested because of the inhuman systems being installed on those borderline securities. There were minefields, spring-loaded guns, and trained dogs. The dogs attacked humans until they ripped them apart. They were taught to ignore a bloody rabbit running through the field but were trained by smell to attack only humans. If you tried to leave East Germany, they wanted to make sure you would die trying.

During my time with the military, I began to doubt the Communist system. I began to criticize many things I saw that were contrary to the ideal picture drilled into my mind during my days of school. We had to endure sixteen weeks of boot camp training, and every week we were on the shooting range twice a day to find the best shooters. The excellent shooters were sent to the borderline, and those soldiers could not miss a person trying to escape East Germany. If they missed, they were sent to military jail. There was no excuse for missing someone because they proved themselves during basic training and passed all the shooting requirements. I had no desire to work at the border so I made sure to fail the shooting ability test even though I knew I could hit the target consistently.

The doubts about Communism began to grow in my mind more and more over. I was still a Communist, but I now only believed it would work if you had the right leaders and people in control. I believed honest people could make it work, and I believed I could change it. I had doubts because what I was taught did not add up with what I experienced every day. It was simply an ideology that sounds good in principal but is actually wicked and corrupt at the core. Finally toward the end of my military career it happened; the events that would change my life forever—or should I say the person who would change my life forever!

★ ★ ★

Christiane was a young girl who grew up in East Germany with her farmer grandparents. She had many relatives in West Germany; unlike me she had a good upbringing where the faith of Christ was a consistent influence in her life. She grew up knowing the evils of Communism from the beginning because she experienced the true life of freedom and peace that comes from a relationship with the Creator of the world.

The events surrounding our meeting will seem like coincidence to some, but it was pure Providence to me. Some of her relatives gave Christiane a car, and while driving one afternoon she was in a terrible accident.

The medical crew immediately took her to the hospital where she was placed in a shared room with an older woman. The older woman was my mother. They ended up sharing the same room for quite some time. I can still remember walking into the room and seeing a long braid sticking out from under the covers in the bed. I did not know it at the time, but the braid belonged to the woman who would later become my wife.

Christiane had a strong faith, and she immediately began to plant doubts in my mind about the relevancy of the Communist system. She began to point out in clever ways the fallacy and evilness of such a way of thinking. I became intrigued somewhat with the information she was presenting to me. I was still a Communist but not as strong as before. In fact, I even purchased a Bible to begin reading about these things she was sharing with me. I have to admit I thought the Bible was foolishness because I did not understand it much. In fact, the Bible itself says that to an unbeliever the Scripture is foolishness, and at least this was a point with which I could agree.

During this time I had a job as an electrical engineer and worked aboard a fishing trawler. Many of those trips were long, especially when we were sent out to the North Sea. We could be gone for months so I had the time to read this strange book called the Bible.

Remarkably, some things began to make sense, so I began to dig into it more and more. When the Bible says, "draw near to God, and he will draw near to you," it seemed to be true. It was happening right before my eyes. I was beginning to believe.

In 1976 Christiane and I were married, and I decided to go to graduate school. In our Communist country you could not just choose to go to school where you wanted, you had to apply with your company and they delegated where you could attend school. Everything in East Germany was planned out for you by the central government. The government education department controlled everything.

Depending on your grades you either ended up in an apprenticeship for a particular trade or you went to some sort of college or preparatory school. The company told the education department what they needed, and they in return told the company where they could send their people for the training.

A file was kept on you for your entire life, and they checked your background to determine if you were an admirer of the Communist system. If you were not, you could not get an education. Because my father was in West Germany, I ended up having to get a special statement from my teachers stating I was useful to society and a proponent of Communist ideas. Without the statement I never would have been able to get my electrical engineering degree from an undergraduate school.

In fact, there was a centralized planning commission once you graduated from school. They told you one of two places you could go. The place you chose was the place you usually had to stay for life. You could not choose to move without government approval.

Because Christiane and I were married, I wanted to progress in my career so I asked the company if I could apply for a graduate degree specializing in advanced electronics. Without the company sponsorship, this would never happen. My grades were not the best so I had to attend a preparatory school before I could go on to graduate school. After graduating second in my class, I went to the company human resources department and had to convince them electronics would be a viable skill for the future, even on fishing trawlers.

They agreed, and in 1977 I was sent off to graduate school some ten hours away from home and family. This was a hardship for me because Christiane was pregnant with our firstborn son. So I applied for a school much closer to home and was denied. I applied a second time and was granted the change. However, instead of going to the Institute of Technology in Electrical Engineering close to my home, they put me into the Institute of Technology and Communications in Berlin five hours away.

It was a well-known institute, but I was not prepared to jump into the second year of graduate school into a different subject. I had several exams I had to take just to catch up. It was tough, but I managed to graduate.

I was married, had a newborn son, and was learning more about the Bible. It seemed to all come together for me one day when I was sitting in a Communist Party meeting. I could not take it anymore. I just stood up and said, "I believe in God, I believe in Jesus Christ, and this Communism doesn't give me anything anymore." I walked out of the meeting liberated. I knew things would be better in my life now. I knew I made the right decision.

I was confident in what I did until two days later when all hell broke loose. The Communists ordered me to be removed from my current workplace, and I was relocated far away from home. Now I was unable to go home every night.

The Communist government forced the company to move me to a more remote location where I was very isolated. They placed eight of us men together in a single room. These were my new living conditions.

I was basically considered a spy because I decided to leave the Communist Party, and a spy did not last long in East Germany. I knew my family's only hope for future survival would be to escape this land of tyranny, but any attempt usually resulted in certain death. Our future did not look good.

As an East German citizen you basically had very few rights. The Communist Party dictated what you could and could not do. This all began to change for me when one day I was going through some files my mother had. I found out my father lived in Vienna, Austria, and was an Austrian citizen. I did not think much about it at the time until I was watching a TV show explaining how a person became an East German citizen.

They said, "It was a bloodline which came down through the father to the children. The father's citizenship determined the citizenship of the child. If your father was East German then you were East German. The other way you became an East German citizen was if you applied to be one." So based on the information they provided I knew I was *not* an East German citizen. I was an Austrian citizen, so there might finally be a way for me to get us out of this Communist nightmare.

We contacted some of Christiane's relatives in West Germany because she had an aunt who traveled regularly to Vienna. We wanted to see if we could contact my father. All of this had to be done in secret. The Communists controlled everything; it was like living in a large prison. If they found out you were trying to get out of the country, they would throw you in jail. Then they would take your children and put them into foster homes of families who were strong Communists.

> *Can the liberties of a nation be secure when we have removed a conviction that these liberties are the gift of God?*
>
> — THOMAS JEFFERSON

Unfortunately we had no luck getting information through her relatives so we decided to go to East Berlin and walk into the Austrian Embassy. It was a five-hour train ride to Berlin. When we got there, we walked in and I spoke to the lady at the front desk. I told her, "I believe my father is an Austrian citizen, and he lives in Vienna. Here is his name and his date of birth. I really need to talk to him."

She looked at me and asked, "Were your parents married when you were born?" I told her I believed so. "Well if your father was an Austrian citizen when you were born, then you also are an Austrian citizen." Christiane and I looked at each other, and we were ecstatic. The lady told us she could find out this information for me. I immediately wanted to know if the East German government got any information about this. She said, "No, this is strictly an Austrian matter, and everything will take place in Vienna." It seemed like a ray of hope began to beam through the windows when I heard her speak those words. I told her to proceed and let's see what happens.

So they began an official investigation, and I had to sign many affidavits. It took the Austrian bureaucrats about two years to find out I was legally and lawfully an Austrian citizen by birth. During that two years' time, I traveled regularly to the Austrian Embassy in East Berlin to check on the status of the process.

From the time I began the process of searching for my father's citizenship, I was under constant surveillance by the Stasi. The Stasi was similar to an all-powerful FBI controlling all the police in the country. They had all the information on what was going on everywhere, and their main objective was to ensure the eternal power of the Communist Party. We called the people who worked for the Stasi, Rubber Ear. We usually said if there were three people standing together one of them was a Rubber Ear. It was absolutely the case; you could not trust anyone, not even people in your own family.

On one particular trip to East Berlin, we decided to take our two children, ages four and five, with us. They would get to see the capital, and we could stay a few days. This way we could get some things we could not get back home. We arrived late into the city and checked into the hotel for one night. You never stayed more than one night in a hotel, or you called attention to yourself. The Stasi would then want to know why you were staying so long in Berlin. So if you planned to stay four nights somewhere, you stayed in a different hotel every night.

Once we got checked in, we went straight to bed because it was late and we were tired. The next morning we had a quick breakfast, stepped out of the hotel, and began the short walk to the embassy. However, things were different; it was strange outside. This was a busy city, and now it was eerily empty. We walked briskly down the road and made the turn down a side street toward the embassy.

The Austrian Embassy stood parallel to the Berlin Wall. As we got about halfway, we noticed two policemen at the end of the street but advancing in our direction. I turned around to see two more behind us, and they were closing in fast.

The whole area was empty, which was not usually the case, and I told Christiane, "Something is wrong. We have to get out of here." We knew we could not outrun them because we had two young children with us. We also knew if they caught us we would be thrown in jail and would never see our children again.

We decided to make a break for the embassy. I was first to the door and hastily rang the bell. Normally they would just open the door but not this time. A small window was opened in the door, and a voice asked me what I wanted. I shouted my name and said, "I am an Austrian citizen." I heard a voice coming from inside saying, "Let him in; he is a citizen." This was the first time I knew I was an Austrian citizen.

I was elated, but then the elation turned to terror as I looked back and saw Christiane and the children coming up the spiral staircase. Our son was in front, and my wife had our daughter under her arm running up the steps. The police were now grabbing at her heel. The lady behind the door yelled out, "The children are citizens too." And they flung open the door, getting my wife and the children safely inside. Divine intervention!

We breathed heavily and held each other. We came close to actually losing everything, including one another. The lady from the front desk came over and explained to me about my Austrian citizenship. She said, "Come with me. We have some papers to fill out." She was not kidding. I had to do a lot of paperwork, then they issued me my passport. I was so happy I slept with it for weeks. I constantly opened it up just to look at it.

Elation soon turned to disappointment when reality set in. I realized even though I had my passport I could not cross the East German border because there was no Visa in it. To the East German government my passport was an illegal document in my possession. I could not just walk up to the border and leave.

I was devastated because I worked so hard to determine my citizenship and held a passport proving it. Yet I was still a prisoner under the Communist system. I yearned for freedom and a better life for my family, but the all-powerful and controlling central government wanted none of it for me. The Communists won.

Years before I met a lawyer who was a great help to me. When I had become a Christian, I did not want to renew my pledge of allegiance to the Communist Party or to the East German army. At the time he told me I needed to because if I didn't it would be treason and I would either end up in prison or shot. He was a man who apparently really cared, so I decided I would go to see him. I really hoped he could help me with my newfound citizenship.

I knew where he lived because he had been working on some cases for the Lutheran church. I decided to go visit him one weekend with my paperwork in hand. He was not there at the time, and his wife was very unfriendly, so I decided I would sit outside and wait for him.

I waited until late into the evening when he finally arrived. He glanced briefly in my direction but went straight into his home. I could hear him inside having an argument with his wife. Shortly thereafter he came out and asked me what I wanted. I told him I needed to talk about a sensitive matter. He was not interested and told me to leave. I turned, shoved the paperwork into his hands, and said, "Read this!" He took it and began to read, then he said, "OK, come into my office."

He told me I needed to get a clarification of my citizenship. He made me five copies of my paperwork and dictated some letters I would need to take to the notary for authorization. Then with a serious look on his face he turned and warned me, "Do not let the originals leave your hands under any circumstance. Do you understand?" I acknowledged, all the while just staring at this copy machine. I had never really seen one before. I had only heard of them. The government strictly controlled copy machines. They did not allow ordinary people to have them out of fear someone would use it to spread non-Communist material. Like I told you before, everything was controlled.

After getting the necessary paperwork, I went to the one notary in our town. When I arrived there were about twenty people waiting outside to see him. I sat down and waited.

After a little while a clerk came and asked me what I needed. I handed her the copies and told her, "I need these certified." She looked over the documents, then said, "OK, give me the original documents." I immediately told her, "No, this does not leave my hand. When he is ready I will come in and have him certify these papers in my presence, but it does not leave my hand."

Like a pouting child, she left and went back into the other room with the copies. A few moments later she returned and said, "The notary has talked to the Department of Internal Affairs, and they want you to come see them immediately."

The Department of Internal Affairs was like the secret police and state security all rolled into one. They are the political leadership of the internal order, and they were in every city. I sat there stunned, knowing a notary, who was the most trusted person in a society, ratted me out to the internal affairs department.

I left with no intention of going to the Department of Internal Affairs office; I headed straight home. I knew if I went there, I would have lost all of my paperwork proving my citizenship.

I went home dejected and wrote letters to all the people the lawyer told me to contact. I had a P.S. at the end of every letter explaining how I tried to have these notarized but was denied. I got the letters ready to mail but decided against sending them from my hometown or place of residence. The Stasi checked certain people's mail. They monitored what you sent and what you received.

By now I was pretty sure they were watching my mail. I decided to take the train to Berlin and mail the letters from there. It was a ten-hour train ride round-trip, but I felt this was necessary. When I arrived I went to several different districts to mail each letter separately. I had to take every precaution I could, my very freedom depended upon it.

The next weekend we traveled to see my mother and my siblings. It was important to me to tell them what I now knew, that they were Austrian citizens as well. When we got there I explained to my sister and brother what I learned. When they heard my news, my sister was very excited, but my brother was not happy at all. He turned and exclaimed, "You are a traitor. What you are doing is treason. I will tell you this, if it ever comes to a fight for survival for the Communist Party I will make sure you are the first person they have shot." There was certainly no brotherly love shown for me.

My brother was a full-time worker with the youth organization of the Communist Party, and it was his job to turn kids into Communists. He took what he did very seriously, and from that day forward he became my staunch enemy. Later on I found out my brother was feeding information about me to the Stasi. He was definitely a Rubber Ear.

After a couple of weeks passed, I finally got a meeting with the government officials to whom I mailed the letters. When I came in I sat at a desk with one man in front of me and two standing behind me. I was told not to turn around, and I could not take notes. They said they were reviewing my case, and because my mother was an East German citizen they decided to make me an East German citizen. I told them, "I am an Austrian citizen by birth. You cannot just make me an East German citizen."

The man behind the desk was not happy with my response. He looked at me and said, "I have a solution for you. If you will give up your Austrian citizenship, we will give you an East German passport. You will then be able to travel anywhere you want." I knew this was phony because I would not be able to get the necessary Visas I needed to leave the country. Disgusted I said, "You are trying to sell me a dog that won't hunt, and this is a bridge that is not solid to walk over."

I did not trust them at all, and I was not about to relinquish my citizenship. I got up out of the chair and said, "You guys lie, and because you have no solutions, I am out of here; I am an Austrian citizen." Emboldened with a new sense of determination, I walked out of the office. I knew they did not want to let me go to Austria. The man had also told me about an international law that applies to citizenship. It says if you have dual citizenship, the country where you reside overrides your other citizenship. I did not know if this was true or not, but I did not want to reside here any longer. I wanted to leave.

I decided the best chance to exit the country was to go back to the Austrian Embassy and ask them what we needed to do. So I took another five-hour train ride to Berlin and went to the embassy. After some moments of discussion, they advised me to formally apply to leave the country. I knew if I did this our entire family would face great hardship, but I felt there was no other choice.

With my background our children would never be able to go to a university. There would be no decent future for our family. The Communists considered us mentally ill because we believed in God, and our children would not be allowed to advance professionally. They would keep anyone out of the best universities and professions when trust was placed in God and not in Communism. It is such a vile and wicked form of government born from the pits of hell.

With help from the embassy, we decided we had to do this. We wrote the application to formally leave East Germany. We had to be very careful with the wording in the letter because if it was worded incorrectly it was a crime and we could spend up to seven years in prison.

Once we got everything together, I decided to deliver the letter by hand to the agency because it was a crime if the letter did not end up in the correct department. We knew it would take about six weeks for us to hear anything; we were on pins and needles.

During this time the lawyer at the embassy advised me to make sure to let my employer know I was applying to leave. If I did not do this, it was a crime and I would do time in prison. We did not know it at the time, but for the next six weeks the Stasi was watching us every hour of every day. They had us under constant surveillance.

The six weeks finally elapsed, and we got our answer. It came in the form of one sentence. "Your request to move to Austria has been denied." I was devastated, but I knew they were supposed to have supplied me with a reason for the denial, which they did not. So I took the train back to Berlin and headed to the Austrian Embassy to see what I should do. He told me to apply again because it is just a matter of time before they give in. He said, "Sorry, it is the best advice I can give you."

So I applied again and was denied again. I was so frustrated by the process, yet I was determined so I applied again and once again I was denied. I was furious so I decided I would go back to the Austrian Embassy, this time to meet with the ambassador.

On the train ride to Berlin I prayed I would get some answer, some relief for our situation. I arrived at the embassy, and I was escorted into an office to meet with the ambassador.

After explaining the situation to him, he told me, "The prime minister of Austria will be coming to East Germany. During that time he usually will give to the East Germans a list of people who should be allowed to leave due to Austrian citizenship. These are considered hard cases, and the request will usually not be denied. I can get you on the list. It is our best chance, and it should work."

I was very excited to hear this, and within a few minutes he had talked to the minister of foreign affairs in Austria. They gave him the green light to put me on the list; I was number eighty-nine. I was then directed down the hall to start the process. It finally seemed like I was getting somewhere.

I stepped into the next office and talked to the embassy lawyer. He told me I had to apply *again* to leave East Germany. He said, "There has to be an open application out there before we can put you on the list, or they will say they don't want to leave East Germany; they have not even submitted an application."

I went home and once again filled out the paperwork to apply to leave East Germany. Three weeks passed and the word came—denied again!

I was so exasperated. I immediately got on a train and went down to the embassy. Furiously I stepped into the office and asked, "How could I be denied again since I was on the list." The man sheepishly said, "It happens sometime; I think you should go and apply again." I was so upset and was so very discouraged. On the five-hour train trip back home I just pondered what else could I do.

The next day I went to work. When I was finished, I got on my bicycle and rode down to the local police station. I went in and asked to see a specific major who was over the police there. It was not a typical office day, but after a few minutes they brought me in to see him. I walked in very bold and said, "As you may know already, I was in the Austrian Embassy yesterday. I want to tell you the Austrian Embassy and especially the ambassador are very disappointed in how the East German government is handling the wish of the prime minister of Austria to get my family to the country where I belong. I can tell you the embassy is working on a note to the foreign department and the internal department of your government expressing their disappointment. I don't know if you or who-ever is responsible for denying us the allowance to leave can take the result of that letter."

Immediately he asked if I was threatening him. I told him, "No, I just want to inform you so you can be prepared for what is coming." I then walked out the door, got back on my bicy-cle, and went back to work. Nothing I said was true, but I was rolling the dice to see what would happen. I had no success any other way so I decided to be bold—or crazy you might say in this instance.

The next day Christiane called me at work, which was difficult because we had no phone. She had to go into town and use a phone booth just to make the call. She was unable to contact me directly, but she was able to contact my boss; and she told him, "I need Harald to come home immediately. It is extremely important." My boss told me I was needed at home, that I should go now. I went straight home, and when I got there Christiane handed me a small postcard that said, "You are required to report immediately to the police station." It looked like my brash talk yesterday landed me in hot water. We would now probably never have the chance to leave this Communist prison known as East Germany.

I looked at Christiane and said, "I must go." I got into the car and drove immediately to the police station. I did not know what to expect, but when I arrived there were about one hun-dred people sitting inside. I walked over, handed the lady at the desk my card, and asked her where I needed to go. She looked at it and told me, "Come this way." I followed her into an office where I was told to sit down.

A piece of paper and a pencil were pushed in my direc-tion. Then she stated, "Write down everything you have to do;

your application has been approved." I was dumbfounded. My brash talk did not get me into trouble; it was the push needed to get my application approved. I could not believe it; I was finally going to get to leave this terrible place.

Within seconds I started making the list of the things we would have to do before we could leave the country. I was so excited to get home and tell Christiane and the kids we would be free. We had to declare the money we had in any bank before we could leave. Usually they would not let you take all your assets if you were leaving the country; however, a nice lady at one of the banks secretly told us there was an agreement between the East German and Austrian government. This agreement would allow you to transfer all your money from one country to the other. Wow, I witnessed another miracle!

As soon as we could we began to sell everything. In a Communist country like East Germany, very few people had a car, so when we went to sell our car we got more than double what we originally paid for it. We were ecstatic to be starting a whole new life in Austria. On July 8, 1985, we flew out of East Germany and into Austria. We finally left behind the wicked clutches of Communism. Unfortunately the destructive forces of Socialism welcomed us with open arms.

Austria was certainly a better situation than where we came from, but we found many of the same problems we experienced under Communism. Socialism penetrated everything in the country; even the churches were preaching a watered downed form of Socialism, where you put your trust more in man than in God. We knew we wanted to get away from this godless socialistic way of life. Everywhere you went you were indoctrinated into this way of thinking. People accepted a heavily controlled lifestyle because they believed the social welfare system was worth it. They simply did not know any better.

We knew the only place we would ever have true freedom was America. We knew we would be able to work and build a wonderful life there. It is a place where we would be free to worship God as we wanted. So one day I made up my mind I was going down to the American Embassy and talk to someone about finding a way to America.

The embassy had two policemen marching outside their doors. They passed one another and kept walking, then turned and came back. I decided when they crossed and walked passed I would run to the door and go inside.

On the first try I managed to get to the glass doors with no problem, and they let me in. I walked up to a Marine and began to ask him some questions: "I have an uncle who I believe lives in the United States. Could you please locate him for me?" The Marine stopped and looked at me as if I had two heads and one of them was crazy. He turned to me and said, "No, we can't find that out." I asked him why, and he said, "Well, do you have an address?" I turned and said, "I would not have asked you where he lived if I had an address. You tell me where he lives." The Marine sternly replied, "If you don't have an address or phone number, I can't find him."

I was shocked; I had never heard such a thing. In the Communist and Socialist countries they know where you live at all times because you have to register with the police. Every policeman anywhere can easily access the information about where you reside. In the United States this was not the case, so I thought, *Wow, America truly is the land of the free.*

After some research I found out my grandmother was born in Allentown, Pennsylvania, in 1891. That inspired us even more, and I was convinced we definitely wanted to move to America. We did not speak English, and I did not feel comfortable at the time with taking my entire family to a land where we did not speak the language. So the entire family started studying and learning English. I also managed to land a job with an English corporation. To assist my work with them, they provided private English lessons for me.

After quite some time we finally managed to learn the language, which couldn't have come at a better time. With the economy in Austria beginning to fail and the increase of radical Islamic terrorism, the time to move to America was here. We went through all of the necessary immigration hurdles and moved to the land of the free and the home of the brave. We found the saying to be completely true. America is the only place where you can truly worship and shamelessly live the Christian faith. It is still the only country where an open Christian world really exists.

When the settlers came to the New World, their first governing document was the Mayflower Compact. The document clearly states they planted this colony, "For the glory of God, and advancement of the Christian faith." It was signed in 1620, and at this writing it has been 393 years since they first agreed on those words. As I sit here today I can tell you I am very happy we live in America. We can work hard, prosper, and just like those first settlers, we can worship freely.

However, there are those who are doing quite a good job in this country of deceiving the people into accepting a socialistic way of thinking. If that happens, then what do we do?

If the people of America forsake their liberty, where would we then go for

freedom?

WHAT SO *Proudly* We Hailed

How could I have been so foolish? How could they have tricked me into singing songs of praise to such a wicked individual? How could I worship a system so vial and corrupt? Thoughts like these were now burdening my soul as my mind journeyed back through my childhood. Innocence and joy were replaced with deceit and betrayal. How do good, hardworking people turn away from morality and decency only to embrace the wickedness of Adolph Hitler and Nazi Germany?

My name is Sonja. This is my story of America.

My story begins with an extraordinary day. My very dear friend of seventy-six years, Lore, would be coming for a visit. We grew up together from the age of three. When she arrived, I was so excited to see her, and we

53

immediately began reminiscing about our time together as kids, our homes, families, and school days.

Moments later, I proudly grabbed our school songbook from off the shelf. Within minutes we were boisterously singing the songs of our youth. We had not sung long before we stopped and, in stunned horror, looked at each other. I turned to her and said, "Oh my God, what have they done to us!" Neither of us could believe what we sang. We started talking about what transpired in our lives growing up in Nazi Germany.

I was born in Nuremberg in the year 1927 to a very loving mother and father. We lived in the city, and my father worked in the local food industry. Germany at that time was coming through a period of transition after the First World War. The treaty of Versailles took away so many of the industrial areas in Germany, and we were going through tough economic times.

In 1921 you would pay seventy-five German marks for one US dollar. Then in 1922 it was four hundred German marks for one US dollar. It climbed to eighteen thousand in 1923, and by November of that year it was one million. By the time 1923 came to an end, you had to spend four billion German marks for one US dollar.

Our economy was in complete shambles. We were now borrowing money from other nations at an alarming rate. Our debt to these foreign countries was skyrocketing. By 1929 the stock market crashed, and the economy totally fell apart. During this time a young leader came onto the scene. He promised to get Germany out of this mess. We were introduced to Adolph Hitler.

Hitler had such an electrifying personality, and the propaganda surrounding his speeches was unbelievable. He spoke to thousands of people at large events, saying, "I will help you, and I will fight for you. I will get you out of your misery; all you have to do is join me." When Hitler began his rise to power, he surrounded himself with the neediest folks. These people were poorly clothed and had little to no food.

Hitler was painted as a messiah, a demi-god, and savior. He would be their champion; he would fight for them, making sure they were treated fairly. His government would take care of them, and he would make sure everything was equal. This group of people began to follow him blindly. He was able to indoctrinate them with the ideals of the Nazi party. They had no clue what Hitler really believed; they just willingly bought into his propaganda and went along with the lies.

In 1933 I was almost six years old and was just truly excited about life in general. One of my friends told me there was going to be a torch march through the city of Nuremberg so I asked my parents if we could go. A torch march was an event where the German army marched through the city by torchlight. People played music and cheered loudly as they passed by.

Because I was a persuasive little girl, I managed to talk my parents into taking me. As we walked through the city I can specifically remember hearing my father say to my mother, "This man will bring us nothing but problems." I remember feeling really scared, but my mother turned to my father and said, "Oh come on; let us try him. Germany is in such a mess. Besides, if it does not work out we can vote him out of office in the next election." It brought me a sense of peace hearing my mother say those words. My father did not agree, yet he did not say anything else about it.

My father was one of the few people in the beginning who saw the troubles Adolph Hitler would bring to Germany. He read Hitler's book, *Mein Kampf*, and my father truly believed he would do horrible things. Hitler was a National Socialist who believed in the removal of the classes; there would be no rich, poor, or middle class—all would be the same.

Unfortunately, just like my mother, many decided to give Adolph Hitler a chance, and in 1933 he became the chancellor of Germany. If he did not work out, they would vote for someone else in the next election, yet there were no more elections; Hitler had them outlawed. The Nazi party did not believe in state sovereignty, and they totally eliminated the rights of the states altogether. Over this time he centralized the power of the government all in the name of security, protection, and prosperity. We were told a lie. Unfortunately we willingly accepted it.

I was a very happy young girl, excited to start school, but little did I know they changed all the books and the new curriculum was updated to prepare our young minds to accept the Nazi propaganda. Not only did we get new books; we got a lot of new teachers—ones trained in the Socialist way of thinking.

We were being instructed to look up to Adolph Hitler because he could make things better for us. They taught us to believe he could do no wrong. Every day we got out the song books the school provided, and we sang songs of praise to de Fuhrer.

It was these very same songs my dear friend and I were singing on the day of her visit, when we realized the terrible ways our young minds were manipulated. I know now how very wrong it is to teach kids to sing songs glorifying the leader of your country. They turned this wicked man into a god, and we were being cleverly instructed to worship him.

Each day I came home from school telling my mother and father all the wonderful things I was learning about Hitler. "Isn't he such a wonderful man? Just look at all the things he does for us!" My parents did not share my enthusiasm. My father especially had a growing distrust of the new administration.

Before I started school, my parents and I listened to the British Broadcasting Company (BBC) on a regular basis. However, after my new instruction began, they did not listen to it in front of me. They feared I would say to the teacher, "My daddy does not agree with the things you are teaching."

They most certainly did not agree with what I was learning in school. Each night after I was asleep they secretly listened to the BBC. From that source they learned the kinds of things Adolph Hitler was doing around the country.

My parents had to keep their views secret. Defiance of the Nazi Party resulted in torture, imprisonment, and, on most occasions, death. My life was so completely different at home than when I was in school. They totally controlled us in school; we did not get to have any of our own thoughts or beliefs. They told us what to believe and who to believe in. From the beginning we were taught the Jewish people could not be trusted, and belief in God was highly discouraged. We were instructed to trust completely in the leader of our country.

Even though I was young, I could see how things in our country did seem to improve. For a period of time the economy did appear to rebound. Apparently Adolph Hitler accomplished putting Germany back on a firm financial footing. This turned out to be nothing but a lie, for the economic recovery was a complete hoax. Hitler was having the treasury print money with no financial backing. He was good at this game of illusion, and he had all the help he needed in the state-run media machine.

Getting any news or information that was not propaganda was extremely rare. Hitler outlawed the big radios people had in their homes. These radios were capable of getting news from outside the country, so he took them away, providing smaller radios people still had to purchase. These units could only receive broadcasts from within the country, so consequently all news reports contained only what Hitler wanted us to hear.

The only newspapers were Nazi newspapers, so the average German was unable to get any other information. The Nazi Party controlled all media communication, and Adolph Hitler was always painted in a most favorable light.

In 1936, I noticed my father was away about every evening, so I asked my mother where he would go. She told me, "Sonja, he is just going down to the local bar to have a beer with the local men and unwind from his work day." This was not an uncommon thing in Germany, and I really thought nothing of it at the time. However, the local bar was not where my father went. He instead went two floors below the bar into the apartment of two Jewish doctors. Each night they quietly got together, listening to the BBC broadcasts coming out of London. They knew what Hitler was doing.

These two Jewish doctors were taking a high risk talking with my father, but they trusted him. At first they were a little leery of him, but after many conversations and meetings together their friendship grew. My father told them they needed to leave Germany immediately. Deep down he knew they must get out, for he saw the writing on the wall and knew what Hitler was doing. They balked at his suggestion, saying, "But we are Germans; we fought in the First World War; nothing will happen to us." No matter how much my father tried to persuade them, they would not listen. They were Germans. They were staying in Germany. That was all there was to it.

Finally, after much discussion my father convinced them to send their sons to England for protection. It was smart advice because after 1938 we never saw those two doctors again.

One afternoon my mother was in the city when she happened to see one of the doctor's wives on the street. Relieved she immediately headed over to talk to her. As she got near, the woman quietly warned her, "Get away, and don't talk to me; you will be in danger." My mother noticed the yellow Star of David she was wearing. All Jews were forced by the Nazis to wear this for identification. My mother decided she would listen and not talk to her even though she wanted to find out how they were.

Guilt by association also meant death by association.

My mother knew this quite well. Every day my parents discussed the wickedness of Adolph Hitler, but never in front of me because to me he was a hero, a person to be worshipped. This is what my teachers taught me at school, and I was a dedicated follower.

Turning ten years old was a special time in my life; I was now old enough to be a member of the Hitler Youth. It was so much fun for me and my friend Lore. We loved having all the other children around us. Singing and playing sports were my favorite pastimes, so when I learned we did these things in the Hitler Youth, I became very excited.

I can still remember the day when I received my uniform; I was so very proud to wear it. As a member of the Hitler Youth we were trained to live quite a healthy lifestyle. Sports were a big part of our daily lives. I loved and excelled in swimming. Our instructors taught us songs about Hitler. Everything we did centered on glorifying this man. I can remember sitting around with all the other children listening to the heroic stories our leaders would tell us about Adolph Hitler.

It is frightening now to think how we all believed the manipulative lies they were telling us.

"Whoever has the children has the future." These were the very words of Adolph Hitler. He did not care if the parents believed in him or not, as long as he had the children. "Youth belongs to us and we will yield them to no one"; it was the unwritten Nazi motto.

My parents had no choice in my education because the government had total control over all schooling. They made sure they were the only option, and their goal was to turn out good little Socialists. I did not realize this at the time, but I found out later the very word Nazi stood for National Socialist German Workers Party.

Yes, Hitler had the children, and he was training up a group of young Nazi Socialists to take over the world. Unfortunately I was a willing and enthusiastic participant.

When you are a child your family life is something very special. I can remember sitting around our home singing folk songs together with my mother and father. This happy memory would change after my induction into the Hitler Youth. Instead of singing the beloved songs we always sang before, I tried to get my father to sing some of the songs I learned from my youth leaders.

My father had no interest in singing worship songs to our illustrious leader. The very thought of this man sickened him. He would look at me and say, "Sonja, you know I am much too old to learn to sing any new songs." This shows the wisdom of my father, for he knew I would tell my teachers if he said he did not like to sing Nazi songs. Because I was still young, I believed him. It was quite difficult for my father not to say anything, but he was doing it to protect us. He was actually keeping us alive.

I of course did not realize how serious the situation was. Cunningly Hitler tried constantly to get the children to open up about their parents. This was one of the tactics he used to rid the country of people who did not follow his warped ideology.

In 1939 my father was drafted as a civilian to work with the food supply chain for the German air force. They trained him in Nuremberg, then in 1940 they moved him to Oslo, Norway, after the German invasion. My father was required to help supply the air force with food. It was a very sad time in my life. I cried terribly knowing I was not going to have my father home with us. Nonetheless, all would not be lost. My leaders told me, "Don't fear. Adolph Hitler will serve as a father figure to you. He will help you and fight for you." Once again this was just more propaganda.

In Germany when a girl got to be a certain age, the Nazis required the mother to leave home and go to work in the war factories. They were experts at removing parental influence from us. They wanted our lives to be totally directed by the government. This makes perfect sense to me now, for they believed the government was more qualified to train and raise children than the parents. They believed children belonged to the city, village, and government.

When I reached the appointed age, my mother was going to have to go to work in the war factory. However, this did not happen because my parents had some friends who opened a screw store in Nuremberg. Since a screw store was technically a war industry store, this meant my mother did not have to go off to the war factory. She would stay home and run the store for them, but more importantly this kept her involved in my life.

Before my father left for Norway, he pulled my mother aside to warn her about the people who would come into the store. He told her, "If anyone comes in asking any questions, tell them nothing. Just act dumb like you really don't know anything." I know it might seem like a strange thing to say, but you must realize the time in which we were living. Everything was scrutinized so this would prove to be some very valuable advice.

My mother began running the store, and she really enjoyed it. I can remember having talks in the evening about what I was learning in the Hitler Youth. She in return would tell about her day in the store. On one particular occasion my mother was in the store as usual when a German officer came in wanting to buy three pounds of screws, one pound each of three different types of screws.

Before my mother did anything else she turned and asked the German officer, "May I please have your requisition order for these screws?" It was a requirement before anyone could buy anything from the screw store to have a requisition order from the government. The officer was offended and said, "I do not need a requisition. I am a German officer." My mother was not budging, so she informed him, "Well without a requisition you cannot get any screws." He became enraged as he exited the store, slamming the door on the way out. This would not be the last time we heard from him.

A few days later the German Secret Service, also known as the Gestapo, came to the store. This was an extremely dreadful thing, for if the Gestapo came to see you it basically meant you would either end up in jail or a concentration camp. My mother was so scared she trembled when he began to speak to her. The Gestapo agent said, "I have been sent here to find out what is happening in this store. You are required to come with me to my office for an official investigation."

> *But a Constitution of Government once changed from Freedom, can never be restored. Liberty once lost is lost forever.*
>
> — JOHN ADAMS

They took my mother down to their office and began asking her several questions. My mother talked about everything except what happened at the store. She told the agent about how my father was in Norway helping to supply food for the German air force. She said how I was in training to become a leader in the Hitler Youth. She basically just gave the guy the runaround.

The Gestapo agent eventually gave up because they could get no information at all from my mother, so they sent her back home. My mother and I both suspected that German officer was probably trying to get the screws to sell on the black market. Because everything was highly controlled by the Nazis, the black market was a great place for people to sell stolen or illegally obtained merchandise.

As my mother made her way back home, she stopped by the post office and picked up a card to mail to my father. In the card she told him the Gestapo picked her up. When my father saw the card he was immediately fretful and said to himself,

"Oh no, what did she say?" He figured she must have said something wrong.

My father took the card to the general he worked under and showed him the message, explaining the situation. Once the general heard everything, he told my father to return home at once. That was music to my father's ears. My father turned and thanked the general.

As he was going out the door, the general said, "Wait a minute, Bochmann, you have never joined the Nazi Party." My father stopped and said, "General, you kept me so busy I didn't have time." The general laughed then smiled, and my father did the same. My father said to me later he knew the general was not a Nazi though they never openly talk about it for fear it could mean their lives.

So many Germans did not agree with what the Nazis were doing, but they were made to go along with it. Their very lives were at stake as well as the lives of their families. I can remember hearing stories of the terrible things people did just to survive during the Nazi time.

The Nazi Party insisted we raise our right hand to the sky and said, "Heil Hitler" when we came into contact with another Nazi Party member. It works much like a salute in the American armed forces except this gesture meant salvation through Hitler.

My father had a way of not giving the "Heil Hitler" salute. He would always make sure he had a book under his right arm when he went into a superior's office. He would walk in and put his right arm halfway up, quickly saying, "Heil." He never fully extended his arm, and he never said, "Heil Hitler." This was his secret way of defiance because my father knew open defiance would lead to death. There was certainly no freedom of speech or bill of rights under these National Socialists.

After getting permission from the general, my father was sent home by plane and immediately he headed to the store to see my mother. When he walked in she was shocked. After a moment of embrace he asked, "What happened at the Gestapo office?" My mother said, "I did not tell them anything. I told them a bunch of stuff but not anything important." So my father figured he had better go down to the Gestapo office himself to see what happened. When he arrived they took him back into the office.

The agent on duty said, "We did not know what to do with your wife. We could not find out anything because she would not tell us anything." My father wanted to laugh because my mother truly played dumb; for once she listened to him.

My father told the Gestapo what happened with the German officer and how my mother was following proper procedure. So my mother was cleared of any wrongdoing, and my father left the office and went home. When I arrived from school my father was there, and I was so happy to see him. I had not seen my father for almost two years, and the tears ran down my cheeks. I could not believe I had him home.

However, my joy would be short lived, for my father would soon have to leave to go back to Norway. Before he left he pulled me aside to talk to me alone. I was now fourteen years old, and I stood before my father in my Hitler Youth uniform with my ribbons and leadership badges. At the time I was a full-fledged leader in the Hitler Youth. I instructed the younger children in the ways of the Nazi time and the virtues of our leader.

My father believed I was old enough to hear the truth so he began to explain to me what Hitler was doing to the Jewish people. He told me how Hitler was having them starved, tortured, and exterminated. My parents always taught me to love and respect our Jewish neighbors, yet everything I was taught in school was always anti-Jewish. My school teachers and my Hitler Youth leaders instructed me to adore Adolph Hitler. I was taught to sing songs to him; I listened to heroic stories about him. I idolized him, and now I found out he was the most horrible human on the planet. I was devastated, but I knew I could trust my father. I knew he would not lie to me. I still get emotional and cry when I think of this interaction with him.

I told my father there is no way I can go back to the Hitler Youth, but he told me I had to for a time. I said to him, "I can't. I can't tell the ten-year-olds about the Nazi time and how it is good; it will be a lie." He told me, "Sonja, you must do this for now. You know what they will do to us if they find out we know about him. We have to do this; our very survival depends upon it." I trusted my father and I believed him. My whole worldview came crashing down before me. I would have to go back and pretend everything was OK; but worse still, I would have to go back and instruct those young kids to worship pure evil.

The war was becoming very terrible for us in Nuremberg. In 1942 the bombings began, and we spent lots of time down in the basement of our apartment building. When I left for school each day I never knew if I would see my mother again. My mother was such an incredible woman. During this time we had little to no food, and because we lived in the city, there really was no way we could grow our own. Everywhere you went people were hungry; some were starving and sick.

Each Sunday my mother closed the store and took a train outside the city. Once she got off the train, she walked to each local farm in the area and asked the farmer if she could work a day in the fields so she could buy a small sack of potatoes from him. She was not always successful, but when she was she boarded the train back to the city holding a pile of potatoes. I can always remember how happy she was when she came into the door carrying potatoes for us to eat.

In the beginning the bombings were quite frightening, but after a while we became accustomed to them for we knew when they would occur each day. The Americans always seemed to bomb during the day and the British during the night. I can remember my mother would put the potatoes on the stove, and we would head down to the basement to be protected. After the detonation bombs ended and before the firebombs began, she would say, "It is time to go turn off the potatoes. Come on, Sonja, we can go eat."

Life totally changed. It got to the point I could no longer attend school. This was a blessing considering all the terrible things I was being taught. By 1945 the city was totally bombed out. On January 2 our apartment was hit; we lost everything. My mother and I went to stay with my aunt. She once again sent a small postcard to my father, letting him know what occurred and reassuring him we were OK.

The postcard arrived in Norway and ended up on the desk of the general's secretary. She called my father to the office and read him the card, "Lost everything, we are alive." This was the first time my father broke down and let someone know how he felt. It was illegal for a German to listen to anything other than what was coming from the Nazis. However, my father was secretly listening to the BBC broadcasts with some Norwegians. He heard on the BBC how Nuremberg was destroyed. Had the secretary been a Nazi, my father would have been in serious trouble.

The secretary looked at my father with such a sad look. She asked, "Oh Bochmann, what will you do?" He looked at her and said, "Well, we will just start over." My father was such an amazing man. He always kept quiet to protect us. My father thanked the secretary and left the office. How hard it must have been for him to be so far away and not able to be there to help us. Of course the Nazis were not about to let him come back; they were losing the war and they needed all the help they could get.

Life for us in Nuremberg was really tough. Each day we had to go down the street to the water works department and carry water back to our apartment. Food was very scarce. You would have thought during all of this time we would have been mad at the Americans for bombing our city; it was quite the contrary, we were mad at Adolph Hitler. My mother and I knew the Nazis had to be stopped, and the Americans were our only hope. We both knew what America stood for: freedom, liberty, and justice for all. We only wished they started the bombing years earlier.

Even though Lore and I were best friends, we never really talked about the Nazi time. We were young girls, and I was always afraid to mention anything to her about how I felt about Hitler. You never could be sure who was a Nazi and who wasn't. Because we both were in the Hitler Youth, it was absolutely plausible we were both Nazis. Nothing could have been further from the truth. It wasn't until after the war we were able to talk about how we both really felt. We both always wanted to, but we could not risk our lives or the safety of our families.

As the war was nearing its end, my father, who was still in Norway, sent a camouflaged letter to Nuremberg. He wrote the letter in a type of code my mother would be able to decipher. The Nazis often opened your mail so you had to be careful what you wrote. They constantly spied on your every move. In the letter my father told my mother he wanted me to have private English lessons. He knew what was coming and felt America would rescue us and defeat this evil Nazi Socialist empire.

English was not a language I ever used much. In fact I focused my attention on learning French. My mother made the necessary arrangements, and every day I was learning to speak, what would later become, my primary language. As I look back it is so amazing how my father seemed to always know what to do. He had great wisdom, and I miss him greatly.

When the Allies arrived in Norway, the Nazis took all the civilians, which included my father and put them in Nazi uniforms. They did this to inflict punishment for what they felt was betrayal. So my father was taken captive and sent to a French prisoner of war camp. He was there for quite some time until he was released and returned to Nuremberg.

We were so glad to see him. He was so skinny; he looked like he had been starved. Because our home was destroyed, my father had no clothes to wear when he arrived so we borrowed a suit from my uncle and fortunately it fit. I did not care how he looked; it was just so good to have him home.

When the Americans arrived in Germany, they set up their headquarters in Nuremberg. This would become the site of the war crimes tribunal. Adolph Hitler and his Nazi cronies were judged for the crimes they committed against humanity. Having the trial in Nuremberg was actually a huge benefit to my family. Taking private English lessons meant I was able to get a job at the tribunal. I was a nineteen-year-old girl who was taught to worship Hitler, and now I would sit in the very courtroom where his Nazi Party leaders would be tried as criminals. In five short years I went from Nazi Youth leader to an active enemy against the Nazi Party.

My first position was with the Russian delegation as a typist. I sat there each day and recorded every instance of what was going on in the concentration camps. I always knew the Jewish people were in those camps, but this was the first time I heard what really happened to them.

Most were forced labor camps and punishment was severe. If any disobeyed they were tortured or whipped. At some camps guards tied the wrists of prisoners behind their backs and hoisted them off the ground. They would then beat them mercilessly. The Nazis killed the young children along with the mothers and older sisters. Little kids were sent to the gas chamber then buried in mass graves. Some Jews were instructed to dig their own graves. Then they would have to stand in front of it while a Nazi soldier shot them. Their lifeless bodies fell into the graves.

Hitler established a legal basis for his acts of brutal inhumanity by creating the Enabling Act, which allowed him to do whatever he wanted. Then he used propaganda and the media to dehumanize the Jewish race. Absolute power corrupts absolutely.

Hearing all this was devastating to me. I never knew what was happening during the war; we had a complete blockage of news. We only knew what they told us.

Tears began to run down my cheek as I wept at what I was hearing. How could I have been so fooled? This man was not someone to be worshipped and glorified; he was evil through and through. Some of the girls there had no clue how bad the Nazis were because their parents told them otherwise. They were so broken when they heard the news. It was such a wake-up call for us all. The media was a willing accomplice with Joseph Goebbels, our minister of propaganda. We were all kept in the dark, and now the light was shining on their wickedness.

I can still remember us sitting there typing. A girl stopped and said, "Listen to this." She then read what she had been typing, and we all began to weep. Then we went on, and it would happen again. It is still just unbelievable what we learned during the trials. None of us would ever be the same.

After my work as a typist with the Russian delegation ended, I moved on to a job in the prosecutor's office. One of the girls who worked with me changed jobs and went to work for a judge. This man was an American, and he came to Nuremberg for the second trials of the tribunal. The judge's secretary left, and I became his new secretary. This was quite a challenge in the beginning. I knew German shorthand; now I would have to learn English shorthand. It actually was not as difficult as I imagined, and I took to the job easily.

I was so happy to be working. Few Germans in Nuremberg had any form of job, so I knew I was very privileged. Judge Harding turned out to be a great man, and he became an important friend to our family. I worked with him for quite a while until he retired and went back to America.

Even several years after the war, life in Germany was quite difficult. Adolph Hitler and his National Socialist regime had destroyed us. The country I knew and loved was no longer the same. Germany was divided into two separate countries. The free nation Allies established West Germany, and the Soviets turned East Germany into a Communist nightmare. Many East Germans were put in cattle cars and shipped out of the country. Russian troops marched through the land, raping women and young girls. Unfortunately many of the victims were raped repeatedly, as many as sixty to seventy times.

The situation was quite horrible. Even though things in West Germany were considerably better and improving, my father knew we needed to leave our homeland. There was no future for us there. We would have to find a new place to live, but where?

My parents and I agreed; we needed to get to America. These people rescued us from the Nazis. Now we wanted to go live among them, but there was a major problem. We could not just immigrate to America. It would require us to have a sponsor, and who did we know in America who could sponsor us? Of course, Judge Harding immediately came to my mind. In fact, it was he who suggested to my father in the first place that we should come to America.

So at the age of twenty-five, some seven years after the war, I moved with my family to America. Judge Harding suggested we come to Cincinnati, Ohio, because of the large German population. We packed the few things we had and made the necessary preparations to sail across the Atlantic. We crossed the ocean in the hold of a freight carrier because we could move our items cheaper this way. We made furniture out of the storage crates.

It was so wonderful coming to America because here we were able to work hard and earn a living. We had very little money, and both my parents got night jobs as cleaners in a department store. Later my mother went to work for a grocery chain, and my father delivered papers. These were not high-profile jobs, but they were opportunities and my parents took advantage of them. My knowledge of both English and German allowed me to land quite a good job with a chemical company.

We were free! We could buy a home, choose where we worked, and own a business. In Germany if you had a business, you had to join the Nazi Party; you had to be a member of the union. In America you were not required to join a political party or a workers union. You had the freedom to become what you wanted. If you worked hard in America, you could accomplish about anything you wanted. I learned very quickly that in America you can accomplish your dreams.

In 1957 I took my oath to this country and became an American citizen. I stood before my new flag, 150 percent American. Tears streamed down my cheeks as I recited, "I pledge allegiance to the flag of the United States of America, and to the Republic for which it stands, one Nation under God, indivisible, with liberty and justice for all." I was so excited and still am, for I went from the evils of National Socialism to the joys of "Life, Liberty and the Pursuit of

happiness."

AT THE
Twilight's
Last Gleaming

The pain tearing through my flesh was like a hot bullet cutting me in half. Cold tile pressed against my face as I lay on the floor screaming. What could be causing such agony? Only moments earlier I was ready for a normal Saturday night. Now I lay in the bathroom vomiting and wailing in distress. Nothing I did relieved the misery gripping my body. As a frigid sweat encased me, I had no clue a life was about to be drastically altered.

My name is Todd. This is my story of America.

★ ★ ★

I tried to ignore it. I kept telling myself the pain would go away soon, but it did not lessen; it only grew in intensity. My wife became concerned as the vomiting went on hour after hour. I tried taking Advil and resting on the bed, but the agony did not subside. My wife was sick with the flu, and I did not want to trouble her, but the pain intensified until I could not take it any longer. She tried to get dressed to take me to the hospital, but she was unable to do anything to help me.

A few hours later screams of horror filled the room as I fell out of the bed onto the floor. The pain was now so intense it paralyzed me. Worried and distressed my wife called our neighbor Jeff to come to the house. By the time he arrived I was in tears, collapsed on the bathroom floor. Luckily Jeff was a big man; he was able to get me to my feet and down the steps to his car. Hastily, obeying no speed limits, he drove me to the emergency room of our local hospital. As soon as we pulled in, he came around to the side of the car to drag me into the ER. A nurse quickly came with a wheelchair.

I was placed on a hospital bed while the nurse plunged a needle into my arm to prep for an IV. The doctor arrived and saw the excruciating pain I was in so he ordered pain medicine shot into my veins. Within moments, the pain lessoned. The effects of the shot soon put me to sleep. The night of terror, agony, and distress was over, or so it seemed.

Minutes ticked away, but it seemed like hours. Then it occurred again; this tearing of the inner flesh had me coming up out of the bed screaming. Quickly a nurse came into the room with a syringe of morphine, injecting it into the tube that ran to the vein in my arm. The pain once again slowly started to ease as the doctor returned.

"I am going to send you for a CAT scan so we can determine what is causing the problem."

They brought a gurney, transferred me over to it then wheeled me down the hall to the imaging area of the hospital. We entered the CAT scan room where I was placed on a very cold table and waited for instructions.

My body trembled as I looked at the machine shaped like a large donut attached to a wall and I was now being slowly moved into the opening. I began to hear the hum and turn of the inner mechanisms. It sounded like something straight out of *Star Trek*. The technician came across the speaker saying, "Breathe in deep. Now hold your breath." This normally is quite easy to do, but it seems impossible when something is stabbing you in the back and making you want to scream. I do not know how long I was required to hold my breath, but it seemed like hours. "OK, you may breathe." I was so excited to hear those words that I gulped in the air like a dog laps his water bowl.

After they completed the scan, I was put back on the gurney and returned to my room to wait for the diagnosis. Finally the doctor came in and gave me the answer. The issue causing me so much pain was a kidney stone, a jagged calcium oxalate stone measuring about five millimeters. It was the culprit, and it was lodged in my urethra, the tube that runs from the kidney to the bladder. It was stuck, and my body was sending immense signals of pain as the kidney began to back up, becoming infected. The situation was turning for the worse, so I would have to be admitted.

The doctor sat down beside me to explain the options available. "Normally a kidney stone will just pass on its own, but this one is quite large and is currently stuck in the inner lining of your urethra. We will keep you under observation tonight; hopefully it will dislodge itself and pass. If it does not, then surgery will be necessary because it is causing great distress to your kidney. So do you have any questions?" I had none; I was just frozen in shock. I shook my head no and the doctor left. This was not at all the way I wanted to spend my Saturday night.

You might think I would have laid there obsessing about this, but I did not. The only thing I could think of was the fact I was starving. I so wanted a hamburger with cheese. At times it is funny how the desire for a certain food can make you feel irrational. All I could think of was how to get this cheeseburger. I knew my wife could not help me; she was sick at home. Our neighbor Jeff who brought me to the hospital left, and I did not have his number handy. I kept trying to think of anyone I could con into getting a cheeseburger to me. Then I remembered a friend who owed me a favor. I reached over to the phone and called him up.

"Hey Marty, this is Todd. I am wondering if you could do me a favor." Now when you call someone at 11:45 at night and ask this question, you are probably going to hear some strange responses—especially when you are doped up on pain medicine. I can only imagine how crazy I must have sounded. However Marty did not seem the least bit surprised; he just replied, "Sure, what do you need?" Like a thirsty man desperate for water, I said, "Could you go buy a cheeseburger for me? I would go myself, but I am in the hospital and no one here will do it." There was a slight pause on the other end, then I heard him say, "Sure, what hospital are you in, and what do you want on your cheeseburger?" Eureka, I struck gold. I was so excited. "OK, here is what I want; get me a single with cheese, lettuce, and mayonnaise. In fact get the combo meal with the fries and a coke. I will pay you when I get out of here. Thank you." He replied, "Sure no problem, I will be there soon." I was so relieved; I waited excitedly for him to arrive.

And I waited and waited; it seemed like hours passed before he finally arrived. When he walked in the door and I saw the little girl with bright-red braided hair on the bag, I was overjoyed. He said, "Sorry it took so long. You forgot to tell me what hospital so I drove to each one to find out. Then I had to sneak in a back way through the hospital to get this to you. They just won't let you in the ICU with anything. I had to do a few things unethical to get in here." Ethics was never his strong point, but right now I did not care—I had my heart's desire in my hands.

After my midnight snack, Marty left and I decided to try to rest. I was still groggy from the medicine so I fell asleep rather easily. After only a few hours, however, I shot up in bed with severe pain. This time it wasn't coming from my back. It was now near the lower part of my stomach. I just knew it was the cheeseburger, and I always heard you should not eat them late at night. I knew I could not call the nurse because I ate a contraband burger and figured I would be in big trouble. I know it sounds crazy, but with all the pain medicine I was on, thinking logically was not in the equation. I just tried to ignore the pain and get some rest.

Sunday morning came, and I awoke to the sound of a nurse bringing me breakfast. She gave me a funny look when she noticed the bag and cup sitting on the table beside my bed. Just as I was about to dig in, the doctor came to tell me not to eat anything. They were going to do another CAT scan to see if the stone moved. Had it not, they would prep me for surgery immediately. The doctor said, "Since you have not had anything to eat since you got here, we can do surgery this morning if it has not passed. You haven't eaten anything have you?" Well, what else could I say? I simply turned my heard and looked straight at the empty fast-food bag. Needless to say, the doctor was not happy; neither was the nurse. Any surgery would have to wait. Did I mention how I *love* cheeseburgers!

Now I lay there wondering and waiting. Seconds became minutes; minutes became hours. All I could do was wait and pray. Then, it happened. The stone causing me so much trouble decided it was time to relocate, and moments later it freed itself. Within the next hour, it passed from me. My terror was over.

Now the good part came. I would get to go home! The doctor came and officially discharged me. He gave me some papers to sign as a nurse removed the IV tubes from my arm. I got out of the bed, stepped out of the door, and headed for the front of the hospital. It would feel so good to leave and put this event behind me. It never even occurred to me I had no way to get home. I certainly did not want to hang around that hospital any longer. Getting out of there was the only thing on my mind; that is, until I heard a voice come over the hospital public address system—a voice I would have normally ignored, but for some reason this time I did not.

"If there is a chaplain anywhere in the hospital, would you please come to the intensive care unit immediately? This is urgent!"

Well, the statement should have had no effect on me. I was no chaplain, no preacher or minister; I was just an ordinary thirty-year-old guy. Yes, I went to church on a regular basis, but these people needed a chaplain, so I ignored the message and headed out the door. However, I heard the message again and the voice seemed more urgent.

"If there is a chaplain anywhere in the hospital, would you please come to the intensive care unit immediately? This is urgent!"

I stopped and thought to myself, *Well, maybe I can do something.* I did not know what I could do, but I felt compelled to go. So within minutes, I was back at the intensive care unit, only this time I was not coming as a patient; I was coming to help someone. Well, at least I had hope that I could help.

Upon arriving at the nurses' station, they looked at me oddly. "Didn't you just get out of here? Are you having more pain?" I explained to them how I heard the message over the intercom. Surprised, the head nurse said, "Oh, we didn't know you are a chaplain." I said, "I am not, but I thought I might be able to help anyway." The nurse replied, "Well, maybe you can. There is a family down the hall whose grandmother is dying, and they have asked for a chaplain to come pray with them. Do you think you could pray with them?" I paused for just a moment and told the nurse, "Yes I think I can." She pointed down the hall to the last room on the left.

As I made my way down to the room, my heart beat extremely fast and intense, as if it was coming out of my chest. *What am I doing? How can I help a family whose loved one is near death? What will I say? What if I mess up?* The questions ran through my head as I walked. Just as I decided I should walk away, I was at the door and the faces inside the room were now staring at me. Running away now didn't seem like a viable option.

"Are you the chaplain?" asked one of the ladies seated inside the room. I swallowed deeply. Not wanting to disappoint the woman, I lied and said, "Well yeah, sort of." A look of relief came upon her face, and she invited me into the room. I was just hoping to not be struck dead with a lightning bolt after my lie.

The room seemed dark, full of despair and sadness. Gathered around the bed of the dying grandmother were seven people—three men, two women, and two children. Their faces were stained with tears because their beloved mother and grandmother neared the point of death. No one seemed to have any peace about what was going to occur; husbands held wives, while mothers tried to comfort children. It was a heart-breaking scene, and I willingly placed myself in the middle of it.

What have I gotten myself into? I am not prepared for this. Why did I come, and what am I going to say? These were the thoughts running through my head. I now wished I'd paid better attention in church last Sunday. Maybe some words of wisdom or comfort would come to my mind, but it was just blank. All I could do was look at the people with compassion and empathy, knowing someday I, too, would be in their position.

One of the ladies broke the silence. "Could you pray for our grandmother and perhaps read some verses out of her Bible? It is there beside the bed. Just read anything you feel would be appropriate for the situation, Chaplain."

Oh no! Now panic really began to set in. OK, I must remember something I could share, something I could read. I had read the Bible many times; now nothing seemed to come to mind, absolutely nothing. Slowly I walked over to the table and picked up the worn black book laying beside her bed. I saw a name embossed on the cover: Viola Watson. This was the name of the lady before me, about to die. The previously anonymous lady now had a name, and the intensity of the situation began to grow in my heart.

As I nervously opened her Bible, I noticed a bookmark. Quickly uttering a silent desperate plea for help, I turned to the marked page and saw the familiar passage of Scripture: Psalm

23. With a sigh of relief and a silent "thank you" for answered prayer, I sat with the grieving family and started reading to them the words from this chapter. It was amazing how it put people at ease. I was very grateful God allowed me to be a help to them.

After reading the chapter, I slowly closed the book, looked at the family members, and said, "I would like to take a moment and pray with you if that is OK?" Each person there responded in the affirmative, and I nervously began to pray. The words I spoke in prayer are not important, and, honestly, I don't remember what I said. I only remember my mouth opened and words came out. Whatever I said seemed to bring a great comfort to those family members seated by the bedside of their loved one. After a few moments, I finished the prayer and began to say good-bye to the family. They seemed quite grateful and thanked me for coming.

Before I left I told them the name of the church I attended and stated, "If you need anything else, just call the church; one of the pastors will be happy to help you." I figured this was the best thing I could do for them—point them to someone more qualified to help with the situation. Once again I bid farewell to each member of the family and a final good-bye to Viola Watson, a name I assumed I would never hear again. Oh, how wrong I was!

I was finally able to get a ride home, and things returned to normal. Monday came and went just like it does every week. On Tuesday I went to the office, worked a full day then headed home. It seemed like a normal Tuesday when I received a call from one of the pastors on staff at the church I attended.

I heard the voice ask me, "Hey Todd, do you know a Viola Watson?"

Bewildered, I stopped my car and said, "Yes I do know her; how do you know her?" The pastor began to explain, "Well a woman called here today to speak to the chaplain who was on staff Sunday night at the hospital. I told her we did not have anyone there. She was undeterred and repeated your name. She said you visited them, and you are a chaplain from this church."

I began to stammer and back-pedal. "Pastor, I never told her specifically I work for the church; I just tried to pray and help them." I was so scared. I was afraid there was some heinous punishment for impersonating a minister. I know they can throw you in jail for impersonating a police officer, but this offense had to be worse.

> *Whereas it is the duty of all Nations to acknowledge the providence of Almighty God, to obey his will, to be grateful for his benefits, and humbly to implore his protection and favor.*
>
> — GEORGE WASHINGTON

The pastor began to reassure me everything was OK, then he said, "Viola Watson has died, and her funeral has been scheduled for this Friday." It brought sadness to my heart and a tear to my eye as I thought about the great distress the family members must be feeling. What the pastor said next transmitted utter terror. "They would like for you to speak at the funeral."

Silence. Nothing came out of my mouth. I could not utter a word; I was petrified by the thought of speaking at the funeral. Sure I spoke with the family the other night, but I had no clue what I said. How could I be any comfort at a funeral?

The pastor said, "I told them you would be happy to share a few words. I hope you don't mind." *No!* is what I wanted to shout, but the word would not come out. How could the pastor do this to me? Weren't they supposed to be of help and comfort? I felt stabbed in the back by this man so I decided to tell him no. There was no way I would go share anything at the funeral. However, when I opened my mouth to let him have it for putting me in this situation, the words "I would be happy to," came out instead. My mouth just wrote a check I felt sure would bounce.

I hardly slept at all Tuesday night; I was so fretful of the upcoming event. I tried to play it off like it was no big deal, but it was a big deal. This is the time people say good-bye to a loved one. This was a sacred event; some amateur shouldn't screw it up. All I could do was whisper prayers of desperation, hoping God heard me.

Wednesday at work was fruitless toil. My mind constantly seemed to be distracted. I looked at my calendar and remembered an appointment I would have to keep, and it was out of town on Thursday. Well at least my mind would have to focus on driving instead of the funeral. I probably would not be able to conduct the meeting very well, but at least the trip would be a diversion.

Thursday came and I headed to my meeting. It was about an hour drive north to an area I was not completely familiar with. I had been there before but not enough to know my way around. I arrived at my destination and went in to meet with some colleagues. My appointment went well, but they could tell I was distracted. I just redirected the conversation when the topic came up. The last thing I wanted to do was talk about the funeral on Friday.

After the meeting ended, I got in my car and turned out of the parking lot. My mind was so disheveled I turned left instead of right. I did not even realize I was headed the wrong way. Fifteen minutes later I realized I was lost. Clearly I was having difficulty thinking straight. I could not even remember what road I was on.

I am normally great with direction, but now I was crossed up and I knew I needed help. I decided the best thing to do was to pull over and ask for directions. I know this goes against my instincts as a man, but I was desperate. Besides, my wife was not with me so who would ever know. As I drove along I saw an apartment housing complex and figured I could stop there.

I got out of my car and knocked on several doors, but no one was home. Finally I came upon a young boy playing in a front yard. "Excuse me young man, is your mom or dad at home? I need some directions"

"No they don't live here," said the boy. "I am staying with my grandma. She is inside, so come with me."

Bingo! The young boy and I stepped inside the home where I introduced myself to his grandma. "Hi ma'am, I have gotten lost and need some directions. Do you think you could assist me?" She smiled and said, "I will be happy to help you. Just tell me where you are headed." I began to tell her what road I was looking for, then after a few minutes of explanation she drew a small map in pencil on a piece of paper. I was extreme-ly grateful, feeling confident I could get where I needed to go.

As I stepped near the door I said, "You have a fine grand-son there, ma'am. Does he stay with you often?" She replied, "No, he is just here this week. His great-grandmother recently passed away. He is staying with me while his parents attend the funeral tomorrow. She was such a dear lady. Everyone just loved Viola."

I froze as the hair on my arms came to attention. I was hallucinating; this had to be a coincidence. Dare I do what I was thinking? Against my better judgment, I asked, "Excuse me, but what did you say her name was?"

"Her name was Viola Watson; did you know her?"

No, it could not be. I had to be hearing things. How was it possible? The name Viola Watson was there before me once again. How could I be lost some sixty miles from home and the one door I knock on is related to Viola? I blanched. I slowly sat down in a nearby chair and looked at the woman. "Viola Watson, yeah, I knew her. I was there the night she lay dying."

Slowly I shared with the woman and young boy the story of how I met her. The grandmother began to cry as she tightly held my hand. We just looked at each other and realized it is truly a small world. I told her, "I will be attending the funeral tomorrow. They have asked me to say a few words. I hope I don't screw anything up."

This dear lady reached over to me and in comforting tones said, "Oh dear, you will be fine. I will pray for you the entire time." Just hearing those words from her brought peace to me. As I got up to leave, she reached over to give me a great big hug. Then her grandson jumped up and with a grin said, "If you are going to be at the funeral, can you give my aunt Julie a message from me?" I nodded, "Sure, what is the message?" His grin widened as he exclaimed, "Please tell her I love her and Tommy says hello."

I told the young lad I would be happy to. I spent a few more minutes with them. The dear grandma gave me a bottle of water for my trip as I headed for my car. Driving home I thought to myself, *No one will believe this story. I was living it and I didn't believe it.* After the occurrences over the previous several days, I began to wonder if I was playing a small part in a large event. My mind wondered, *What is going to happen next?*

★ ★ ★

Friday arrived, and I was more nervous than ever in my life. I had no clue what I was going to say. I just kept telling myself, "Do not tell the joke about what is the difference between a funeral and a wedding. One is the end of life and one is the end of the good life." That certainly would not be a good thing to say. Why could I not think of anything but that crappy joke, and why had I not been looking stuff up in the Bible or in a book somewhere?

What an idiot! I kept thinking. However, I knew I had to go; I promised little Tommy I'd deliver his message to Aunt Julie—at least there was one thing I had to say. At this point, it was the only thing I knew I was going to say. Anything else was yet to be determined.

The time came for me to go. My wife tried to reassure me, but I wasn't buying it. I just decided to suck it up and get ready. I put on my best suit, put on a tie, and got in the car. The drive to the funeral home would not take long, and I kept trying to conjure anything good I could share. When I finally arrived I met with the pastor performing the funeral. He told me the order of events and when I would speak.

As the funeral began I made my way to the front of the sanctuary and sat on the platform. The body of Viola lay in a casket directly in front of us. I noticed I would be looking directly down at her when I got up to speak. This was not the most comforting thought. A lady came and sang a touching special song. A few words were spoken by one of the family, then the pastor shared loving thoughts about the life of Viola Watson. Unfortunately his words appeared to fall on deaf ears as all the family members seemed to be overcome with grief.

How would I be able to help them when the pastor in all his wisdom didn't seem to be getting anywhere? My nervousness level was on a steep incline.

As the pastor finished his message, he turned to me and said, "Now, I would like to have a dear friend come up and share with you a few thoughts."

Oh no, it was my turn. Slowly I stepped to the podium. I noticed Viola lying below me, and I felt I was staring at her. I realized how sweaty my hands were when I grabbed the podium. Then miraculously I opened my mouth and words came out. I told the story of how I met Viola and the family at the hospital Sunday night.

It was interesting; the people began to rouse from their grief. It was as if a spirit of comfort and peace began to fill the room. I quoted no scripture, said no prayer, and yet my words seemed to be helping. I continued to speak, then right in the middle of a sentence I stopped speaking and said, "Excuse me, where is Julie? Would she please raise her hand?"

Within seconds a grieving lady seated in the front row next to a large weeping man raised her hand. I locked eyes with her and said, "I met a young boy the other night named Tommy. He wanted me to tell his aunt Julie he says hello. He also wants you to know he loves you very much."

Tears seemed to spring from the woman's eyes as she sobbed heavily and the large man beside her held her close.

Oh no, I screwed up royally. The man shot me a look communicating serious trouble. I determined right then I would beat a hasty retreat with my last words. I was not going to stay around to get thrashed at a funeral by a grieving man twice my size.

I quickly ended my message and walked off the platform. I did not stop until I got in my car; I put the key in the ignition and drove off. My involvement in the life of Viola Watson was over. I was never more wrong.

Six days passed and my life was back to normal. I spent an uneventful weekend and was into a productive week at work when I received a call from a friend. "Hey Todd, could you help me pass out some flyers in our neighborhood on Thursday? We are having a special event at church, and I sure would love some help." I agreed and told him I would meet him Thursday right after work.

Thursday came and it was a beautiful day. People were sitting on their porches, working in their yards, and enjoying the sunshine. I met up with David, and we started passing out the flyers. It turned out to be a relatively easy task. People were receptive, and I enjoyed the interaction.

Things were going smoothly, when David turned and said, "We would get done sooner if you took one side of the street while I work the other." I agreed and started on my way. I had just left one home and came up to the next when outside in the yard I saw two ladies talking enthusiastically. One lady was tall and very slender; the other was shorter with a bright blue shirt on. As I got closer I caught pieces of their conversation.

I overheard the tall slender lady say, "Yes, she had it all planned. She was so devastated she felt like she could not go on. Her and Jack were at each other's throats, then when the death occurred she felt like her life was over." The lady in the bright blue shirt replied, "Wow, that is truly amazing. What caused her to change her mind?"

I hated to interrupt, but I figured I would just hand them a flyer and quickly be on my way. I said, "Excuse me, ladies, I'm sorry to interrupt—" Before I could finish the sentence, the ladies stopped and stared at me as they would a ghost.

As I opened my mouth again, one of the ladies said, "You . . . you are the man from the funeral, the funeral for Viola Watson!" *Not again!* How could this be? What was happening? Was this a joke? Was I going to be forever haunted by the name of Viola Watson? I almost asked them if someone put them up to this but thought better of it. Then the tall slender lady exclaimed, "You are the man who spoke at her funeral; you are the one who saved Julie's life. You are the man, aren't you?"

I nodded my head, but I was confused on the part about Julie. Yes, I spoke at the funeral, but I didn't save anyone's life. *The Twilight Zone* theme music started playing in my head. I decided I would ask for more information, and what I heard next sent chills down my spine.

"Well you see, Julie and her husband were having issues, then her grandmother died. Viola was like a mother to her. She practically raised her from the age of seven. Julie was in such a state of heartbreak she was going to commit suicide. She had it all planned for after the funeral. She sat there thinking about it the entire time, then you called her out.

"She told me it was like she was being shaken out of slumber. So when she slowly raised her hand, she was not sure what was happening. Then when you told her Tommy said to say hi to his aunt Julie, she began to doubt her decision; when you told her Tommy loves her very much, she totally broke down.

"The message of love from her nephew Tommy saved her life; it totally changed her. She told me she knew she could not take her life now for the impact it would have on her nephew. Julie thought Tommy would then think she hadn't loved him. So your message and the love of that little boy kept her from ending her life."

The woman paused then looking straight at me said, "Your message from Tommy saved her life. How did you know it would help her? How did you know what to say?" I was speechless and didn't know what to say. Something bigger occurred and I was part of it. I just stood there and said, "I don't know, but someone knew what she needed."

I have read about how our Founding Fathers believed America was a nation presided over by God, as if the hand of Providence was directing events. In 1787, Benjamin Franklin at the Constitutional Convention stated, "I have lived, Sir, a long time, and the longer I live, the more convincing proofs I see of this truth that God governs in the affairs of men. And if a sparrow cannot fall to the ground without his notice, is it probable that an empire can rise without his aid?"

Is it possible that my pain and suffering led to a woman's life being saved? I know some people would call this a coincidence, but I call it *Providence.*

WHOSE BROAD
Stripes
and Bright Stars

One might say our meeting was one of chance, but we both knew better. I stole $223,000 over the course of only four days. He had been dealing cocaine since the age of fifteen. Our face-to-face meeting resulted in a powerful new alliance. Partnerships like these usually lead to tragedy, but ours is actually a tale of triumph.

We are S.O.G. This is our story of America.

My name is Kyle, and my story of America begins in Jacksonville, Florida, where I was born in 1983. My mom was a single mother doing the best she could and trying to raise a young boy. I was about four when she met a nice man she would marry. He would become the only dad I ever knew. They were not married for long before my mother got pregnant and had another child.

I now had a brother to grow up with. My brother and I had two parents who worked very hard to give us everything we needed as well as most things we wanted. You could not find a more loving and supportive environment in which to grow up.

For the most part, my childhood was uneventful. Sure I had some difficulties but nothing out of the ordinary. I was a good kid and very thankful for my upbringing. I was truly a blessed individual. When I graduated high school I went off to college, which my parents graciously paid for. I had everything going for me, and there was no way in the world I could fail. However, failure did come and it started ever so innocently.

I was on my own for the first time, and I was the one making all my decisions. I began to develop a spirit of ingratitude. I was just not thankful for what I was given. This might seem like a small thing, but it led me down the road to a life of irresponsibility.

I began to acclimate to an unhealthy college lifestyle. I quickly followed the blueprint so many kids do when they first arrive at college. I partied, did not go to class, stayed out all night, and basically just lived large. It all seemed innocent at the time, and I felt so alive. The party ended, however, when I flunked out of college in my first semester.

Because college did not seem to be appropriate for me, my army veteran father suggested I go into the military. So in March of 2002, I enlisted in the army and was sent to Fort Jackson, South Carolina. I really took to the service, which surprised me considering the problem I was having with wanting to do my own thing. I enjoyed what the army taught me. I began to get interested in computers and became a tech geek. Even though I was doing well in the service, deep down I still had the same mentality I had in college. I clung to the idea I could do what I wanted, when I wanted, because I was on my own.

It would not be long before I started doing the same things I did in college. I began to party and get drunk quite often. By the time the army transferred me to Fort Bliss in El Paso, Texas, I was already secretly out of control. One night I decided to sneak across the border into Juarez, Mexico, for a night of revelry. The alcohol flowed freely, and before long I was getting drunk and causing trouble. I was a man with no self-control.

My time in the army lasted about two and a half years, then I got out. While I was in the service I met a girl and fell in love. Everything seemed perfect. I asked her to marry me. She accepted, and as a newly engaged couple we decided to move together to New Mexico. I tried college, and it turned out a failure. I tested the waters of the military for a while, which had also turned sour. So maybe our engagement and pending marriage would be the thing I needed to cure me of this rampant irresponsibility ruining my life. All I had to do was be a responsible man who provided and protected the woman he loved.

Nevertheless, I did not change, and no woman wants to marry a man who is an irresponsible drunk who stays out partying all night. So it seemed this, too, would not work out for me. We decided to end the engagement, and I left New Mexico. My parents knew I was drifting, and they wanted very much to help me. They suggested I return to Florida. I knew deep down it was the right thing to do, but my pride and selfish desires won out. I convinced myself they only wanted to control me and tell me what to do. I was my own man, and I made my own decisions so I moved back to El Paso, Texas. I had friends there and they understood me.

I contacted a buddy of mine, and we decided to get an apartment together. For the most part things went well. We were both living large, chasing women, and partying hard. We were two irresponsible guys living the life of drunks. I knew what I was doing was wrong, but I really had no willpower to quit. Honestly, it was actually quite pleasing to me so I just continued living this destructive lifestyle, not caring where it would lead.

One day while I was at the apartment I went out to get the mail and found something that did not seem like it was ours. I opened the envelope, and it contained a check for one thousand dollars. Unfortunately the check was written out to someone else. My conscience told me I should contact the person who sent the check, but I had long since quit listening to that little voice in my head. Quickly my mind devised a better plan, and this plan would make me rich.

I looked at the information on the check, examining every bit of it. I saw the name, the address, phone number, and most importantly, the account number. I had everything I needed to make this work. I picked up the phone and contacted the bank from where the check had been issued. A nice lady on the other end of the phone answered and asked if she could help me. She sounded a little nervous, as if she was new, so I used it to my advantage. I told her my name, but it wasn't my name; it was the name of the person who issued the check. I calmly said, "Here is my account number. Can you please let me know my current balance?" She verified my account number and address; of course this information was listed on the check so I had it readily available. After a few moments she came back and said, "You currently have $360,000 available. Can I assist you with anything else?" Bingo! I was now in business.

I told her I wanted to make a wire transfer to another account. After a brief pause, she gave the information I wanted. She would fax the necessary form, and once I completed it, I would then have to fax it back to her. I provided my fax number and waited for the document. Minutes later I had the form in hand, and I nervously began to fill it out. In about ten minutes' time I had the document completed, the signature forged, and it all faxed back to the bank. My insides were churning, and I was scared to death. I knew what I was doing was wrong, but I did not care. This was my opportunity for some easy money, and I was not about to let it pass by.

In about ten minutes I got the word. Forty-seven thousand dollars had been transferred into my personal account. I could not believe it worked. I should have quit there, but greed began to take over.

Two days later I tried again. It worked before; I was sure it would work again. This time I decided to up the ante and put the wire transfer in for $88,000. Same routine as before, and minutes later the money was in my personal account. I could not believe how easy this was. After another two days I transferred another $88,000 from the other account to mine. Now, in under only a weeks' time, I went from no money to more than $223,000. This was certainly making money the easy way, and I concluded it was now time for a lifestyle change.

The first thing I did with my newfound wealth was go down to the local car dealership where I bought a Cadillac Escalade EXT for $38,000; naturally I paid cash for it. It was a sweet ride but not totally complete. I needed to pimp this ride so I bought fancy rims and a kicking sound system. For days I rode around in my new sweet machine. I was certainly turning heads and felt awesome but still incomplete. I was not satisfied so I bought another vehicle. This time I would go for the best money could buy.

I strolled into the Hummer dealership and paid $63,000 in cash for a brand new H2 Hummer. Naturally I had to upgrade the rims to a set of spinners and a top-of-the-line sound system. In just a couple of days I spent almost $100,000 on two rides. I was living the dream.

Now I was ready to hit the town. I was the king of El Paso. I spent every evening at the nightclubs. I was doing whatever I wanted. Each night, I walked into whatever bar or nightclub I desired and spent $10,000 living it up. I bought alcohol for myself and anyone around. The women flocked to me, and they were easily bought as well. I was a man wasting my money on riotous living. I was miserable. I could not understand it. I had everything I wanted, yet I was not satisfied. Something was glaringly missing.

For twelve days I lived the life of the rich and famous, then it all ended when a knock came at my door; it was the police. They discovered my theft. Needless to say I was arrested. Actually, it wasn't difficult to track me down. I mean after all, the bank did have the information on where the money was transferred. All they had to do was find the owner of the account then come and get me. When I think back about it, I was truly stupid to even think I could ever get away with such a thing. I was so irresponsible, and it came back to haunt me.

I was charged with aggravated theft. When the indictment came down, the charge carried a first-degree felony. My lawyer told me the sentence was a minimum of five years and a maximum of ninety-nine. I was anxious and terrified. This life of living the way I wanted and being on my own turned into misery. I totally screwed up. I thought about how my mom and dad worked so hard to raise me right. I thought about how they sacrificed so I could have a good home and education. I knew I let them down. What was going to happen to me now?

As I sat in the county jail, I thought about the previous two weeks. I stole $223,000, and now I was looking at several years in prison. I traded fancy cars for iron bars and a striped jumpsuit. The life I knew was over. The new life I was about to acquire scared me to death. There was no way out and I had nowhere to turn.

What I am going to tell you next might seem strange to some and interesting to others, but it is exactly what occurred. A guy I had never met and one whose name I would forget strolled over to me in the cell. He looked kindly toward me and said, "Hey, would you be interested in going to the jail church service?"

Now I can tell you it had been a long time since I was last in a church, and where I attended was nothing but a giant fashion show. Because I had nothing else to do now, it seemed like as good a time as any so I agreed to go. I really did not know what to expect. I just felt compelled to go and listen. The room was nothing special, and the man who stood before us was not even a preacher; he was a construction worker. What in the world was I doing sitting in a church service listening to a construction worker? Certainly I had better places I could be, right? Oh yeah, I was in jail; I had nowhere else to be, so I listened.

The story was one I had never heard before. He told of the Creator of the universe. How He had a son who came and lived among man. He told us the story of Jesus. What compelled me more than anything else was the fact someone would die for my wrongs. I didn't even want to pay for my wrongs. Why would the Son of God want to do it for me?

When the service was over I headed back to my cell and asked to have a Bible. I began to read everything I could about this Savior of man, and on October 6, 2005, I put someone else in control of my life. I turned it over to Jesus Christ then prepared to accept my punishment from the court.

Now I am sure you have heard many a story in your day of some guy who gets locked up in jail and suddenly decides he will trust in God. Well, it is true prison will make you rethink your life, and sometimes the uncertainty of your life's destination will change you. However, some people only change for a short time, and it's nothing more than a jailhouse conversion, which basically means it doesn't last. I had no clue if the decision I made would last into the future; I only knew I needed to change the present. Things in my life were going to detour in a way I never could have imagined.

The day came, and of course I was found guilty—no surprise there. The judge sentenced me to four five-year sentences, but they would run concurrently so the longest I would serve was five years. This was somewhat of a relief not to be going away for longer, but still five years of my life would be gone because of my irresponsibility. After sentencing, I was sent to prison in Abilene, Texas. I was there for a short time before I was transferred to El Paso where I resided in the Sanchez Unit Texas State Prison, my new home for the next several years of my life.

Every day brought the same routines. I no longer had my freedom, and the life of living the way I wanted was over. No privacy, no family, no real friends—only punishment and restitution. The only thing I had was this newly acquired faith, and it was about to be tested in a way I could not have foreseen. I started down a whole different path, and it all began when I met Jeremy, a convicted drug dealer.

My name is Jeremy, and I was born in Lubbock, Texas, in 1979. My home life was much different than Kyle's. I had a mother and a father, but my dad was not around much at all; he just popped in and out of my life. My mother on the other hand was faithful and a hard worker. Between her and my grandma, they did the best they could to raise three kids. Times were very tough for us and we struggled financially. My grandma worked two jobs, and my mom put herself through school. They did anything they could to try and give my siblings and me a better life.

When I was about six years old, my dad decided he wanted to be more involved in my life so he came around more. In a normal situation this would be a good thing, but for me it turned out to be very unfortunate. He would come by the house, pick me up, and take me with him on one of his adventures. My dad's idea of adventure was not a walk in the park or a hike in the woods. It was a trip to the liquor store and then a stop to buy drugs. His favorite pastime was getting drunk and smoking marijuana. My innocence was cut short all because my dad introduced me to his corrupt lifestyle. His father, my grandfather, was actually one of the drug kingpins back in the late 1970s. What a legacy I inherited.

In was not uncommon for my dad to take me with him to drug parties. I spent the entire night running around someone's house with absolutely no supervision. Everywhere people were doing drugs, getting drunk, and having sex all out in the open. Being so young at the time I did not understand what was going on; I only knew I got to do what I wanted while I was there because no one cared.

During my most formative years, I was growing up in two very different realities. My mother provided a loving and caring home full of structure. Life with my father was much different. It provided pure wickedness. I was coming to a point in my life where I would have to choose one of these realities. Like most boys, I decided I wanted to be just like my dad; I wanted to follow his example. Unfortunately I watched his life way too close.

Oh, I wasn't a bad kid, but I would most certainly push the envelope. This rebellious spirit continued up until I was about the age of fourteen; it was then I began hanging with the wrong group of "friends." I was always told, "You are who your friends are." Well my friends all smoked marijuana and drank alcohol. So needless to say, I did the same. Smoking weed for the first time really did not seem like a big deal, but it would lead me down a road I never wanted to travel.

The statement, "Marijuana is a gateway drug to harder drug use," is most certainly true. I soon learned smoking weed was not an innocent thing. I should never have messed with it at all. In fact, I did not even like the way it made me feel; it relaxed me too much. I just started smoking it because my friends were. I wanted to be cool and fit in. Boy, was I stupid.

When I was fifteen I was spending some time with one of my cousins, and I discovered he not only used drugs, but he also sold them. He had a fancy sour apple green painted Cutlass with thirteen-inch gold rims. Everyone loved his car, including me. I asked him how he was able to have such a fancy ride, and he replied, "It's easy. I made the money from selling drugs, and you can do the same." I know now I should have said no, but the temptation was too great. So I gave in and he showed me how to sell marijuana.

I could not believe how easy it was to sell weed. I never had to work very hard to get buyers; often times they sought me out. The money came pouring in, and now I had the bling, the girls, and the image I thought I wanted. I totally bought into the lie of the world of drugs, and because I did, it opened the door for something much harder. I was well on my way to being a serious drug dealer, and I was only fifteen years old.

When you are a drug dealer, you are also a drug user, and I was no different. Marijuana became my gateway drug to something harder. I began to experiment with cocaine after some peer pressure from my cousin. I was familiar with the drug because I saw my father use it. So when my friends put a line of white powder out on the table in front of me, I already knew what to do. After the first use I was addicted, and within six months I was using cocaine daily. The high and euphoria of it just helped me escape. Before long I was smoking the rock form of it as well. I was so messed up I had to smoke weed to help balance out the high I was getting from the coke. I was using a cocktail of drugs each day just to be able to function.

Living like this was bound to be noticed, and my mother took notice. I had always been a straight-A student, but my grades began to fall. When she found out the source of my trouble was drugs, she immediately sent me to rehab. It was a touch-and-go thing because I really did not want to change, but I went through the course and received my completed certificate saying I was "fixed." However, I was not fixed, not at all. For the next seven months I managed to stay clean, but the desire was still there. It was not long before I returned to hanging out with my old friends. The drug habit was back. Cocaine and I reestablished our relationship on a higher level.

When you are on drugs, you do things you would not normally do. I needed a way to finance my habit so I took some checks from a friend's home and cashed a few of them. I was busted and put on probation. Time and time again I did the wrong things. I skipped school so often it resulted in me being held back from my graduation.

I wanted to be responsible, but I could not keep from making bad choices. So in an effort to get my life cleaned up, I went back to rehab. I felt awful because I was going through this again. I also felt ashamed to see the same instructor who was there with me before. However this time I paid strict attention and wanted to make sure I did something different with my life.

After graduating from rehab again, my life seemed to finally be on the right track. I was living right. I was on the straight and narrow. But this only lasted about a year and a half. Soon I was back with my old friends. They truly were reliable, for they always supplied me with cocaine as soon as I showed up. Obviously, it was becoming a vicious cycle. Ever since I was fifteen years old I was doing drugs, going to rehab, and trying to live right. This was my routine for six years of my life. I was almost twenty-one and knew something would have to change. I was ready to break out of this lifestyle; I just did not know how to escape. I thought I was ready for anything, but I was not ready for what occurred next. A joy ride with no joy.

★ ★ ★

It was hard being on probation and trying to stay out of trouble while you are secretly doing and selling drugs on the side. Cocaine was not my only vice; alcohol was its close companion. It was not uncommon for me to spend the day doing drugs or getting drunk. I never thought of the consequences, only about the high I was getting in the present. One day I had been drinking heavily, and before long I was extremely drunk.

I always felt I had my drinking under control so I thought nothing of getting in my car and going for a drive. I grabbed the keys and headed down the dusty dirt road near my friend's house. The road was narrow but good for travel; besides I probably would not run into any cops going this way. The road must have been smaller then I remembered because I decided to drive off the road and into the ditch.

My state of inebriation stranded me. My car was definitely stuck, and there was no getting it free. Here I am drunk, stranded beside the road with my car in a ditch, and I had no clue what I was going to do. I had to find some way to contact someone or a new way to get back home.

I looked across the road and in the field was a large tractor. I figured if the keys were in it I would "borrow" the tractor and drive it home. As I walked up to this mammoth machine I noticed to my pleasure there were keys inside. I had my new ride. I climbed into the seat and started it up. It did not matter to me I had never driven a tractor. I was drunk; I believed I could do anything. Within minutes I had the beast on the road and headed home.

This was not your small, run-of-the-mill backyard tractor; this was a large farm tractor—the kind used in the grain fields of Texas. I was so clueless about what was really happening. I did not even notice it had a large boom on the back of it, the kind of boom they used in the fields for cutting. As I plugged along in my new ride, the boom was swinging behind me and slamming into telephone poles. I don't know how many of those I took out, but they were crashing to the ground as I made my way home.

Because I was drunk, my driving was erratic, and I ended up going into ditches on several occasions. At one point I hit a ditch so hard it popped a wheel off the rim. After that, I was driving on three tires and more or less dragging the fourth. The off-balance position caused the boom to swing around and smash through the back window of the tractor.

"Oh no, they are shooting at me!" is what I yelled as I ducked my head. No one was shooting at me, but I was plastered and I knew for certain someone was trying to take me out. I finally managed to get the tractor near enough to my home to call my mother from a nearby phone and have her come get me. I made sure as I exited the tractor to wipe off any fingerprints. It would not be good for me to get caught; I was hoping no one would notice the tractor was gone. If a person did not see me take the machine, the debris of telephone poles and fences I left behind would surely let them know.

I met up with my mother and we headed home. Of course I told her nothing about what occurred. For the next week everything passed by for the most part rather uneventfully until a knock came at the door. Yes, it was the police. They took me down to the station and began to interrogate me. It didn't take long before I confessed to the entire mess. I was immediately locked up, but I did manage to make bail. Because I was on probation I knew this would not go easy for me.

My life had certainly been spiraling out of control for some time. A few years previous I met a girl who became very important to me. She persistently tried to get me to turn my life around, but I did not listen. I had good women in my life who were trying to help me—my mother, my grandmother, and now Marcia. We had been together regularly, and now she was pregnant with our first child.

This is not the way to bring a baby into the world. I was a drug-dealing thief headed to trial with a baby on the way. Not only had I screwed up my life; it looked like I was about to screw up the life of someone totally innocent. I could only hope the trial would go well and I would not end up in prison.

The trial did not go well, and I was sentenced to eighteen months in prison. I was losing my freedom, and worse still, I would not be there to see my first child born. These were the consequences of my actions; I was reaping the "rewards." I knew prison was going to be difficult.

> *No People can be bound to acknowledge and adore the invisible hand, which conducts the Affairs of men more than the People of the United States.*
>
> — GEORGE WASHINGTON

After trial I was taken into custody and placed in the local jail before being sent off to prison. I spent a few months there, and it was during this time I started remembering a lot of what my mother and grandmother taught me when I was young.

My grandma was a good, God-fearing woman. Through her I knew all about God and I believed Jesus Christ was real, but I had no relationship with him. So I did what a lot of guys do when they are behind bars; I sought out help from God and was willing to bargain. You know how it goes: *I will be good and do whatever you want me to do. Just let me have the one thing I want.* Well the thing I wanted most was to be able to see my child being born, and needless to say this would take some doing.

It is funny how things work out. To most inmates the sheriff is the enemy, but this was not so in my case. It was much like the story of Joseph in the Old Testament; I had favor with the man who ran the jail. Sheriff Jake took a liking to me from day one, and he allowed me to make regular phone calls to Marcia. It was getting close for the baby to come, and she could be in labor any day. Every hour I became more anxious and extremely nervous.

Waiting for my first child to be born was nerve racking. Knowing I couldn't be there because I was in jail was heart breaking. Another day rolled around, and once again I asked Sheriff Jake if I could call and see how things were going. As always he graciously granted my request. I dialed the number, and when Marcia picked up the phone, she exclaimed, "It is time! My water broke. I am heading to the hospital."

The day finally arrived. I quickly hung up the phone and asked Jake if there was any way I could go to the hospital. He turned and said, "Do you have a ride?" Right then and there I called my mother, and before I knew it she was at the jail. Jake walked me to the front door. He shook my hand and sent me on my way—no guards, no cuffs, no constraints of any kind. This was so totally *not normal*, especially in Texas. I felt like Otis in an episode of the "Andy Griffith Show." God worked this out—well, at least in my mind it was God. I mean, I made a bargain with him and he kept his end of the deal.

My mom raced like a NASCAR driver to the hospital, and we arrived just in time for me to see my baby girl enter the world. It was such a bittersweet moment. I knew I loved her and wanted to be with her, but I knew I had to go back to jail.

After a few blissful moments holding my baby girl, I headed back to my home of incarceration.

When I got back, Sheriff Jake congratulated me on the birth of my first child. This man trusted me. He showed me grace when I did not deserve it. The good feeling would end prematurely, for soon after I was sent to prison. I went from feeling as if I was in the heights of heaven to what seemed like the depths of hell.

Time in prison goes very slow, especially when you want to be with your newborn child. Somehow I managed to keep my sanity, and finally the day came for my release. I was so excited to go home. I could not wait to begin a new life with Marcia and our new daughter. This time I knew my life would be different. I was on a new path. God kept his promise to me so I had to keep up my end of the bargain.

Marcia and I were married in 2003. I was more determined than ever to be a good man and father, and for a short time I was. But as before, my old friends came calling and I had no willpower. I was soon hanging out with them and enjoying the nose candy they readily supplied. It was not long before I was totally addicted and intertwined yet again in the drug culture. Soon I became a major player selling drugs in our area.

I was the man; I was the one making the money and calling the shots. I even got my sister involved just to keep things all in the family. I knew the drug-running business, and I was good at my job. I was so good the Feds set up a sting operation. For six months they watched me, then on the appointed day they busted me. I was going down, and they were going to make sure I went down hard.

When all was said and done, they leveled seven indictments against me and I was looking at a sentence of forty-five years to life in prison. My life was over. My selfish irresponsibility ruined it all. I went to trial and, of course, was found guilty. Now the only question was, how long I would spend in federal prison? I was sent away to await the final verdict for my sentencing.

Looking back I actually believed I had been doing everything right in life. It is hard to fathom all the stupid choices I made. Every time I did something wrong and got caught it would break my heart, but it never broke my spirit. Now I was looking at going away to prison for a very long time. Not only did we have a daughter, but now we also had a son. They would grow up without their father in their lives. My heart was truly broken, but this time so was my spirit. There was no pride left in me; I was totally fragmented, right where I needed to be. Actually it is where God needed me to be so I truly could be fixed.

The time finally arrived; I knew I had to surrender my life to God, so I just told him to take control. I knew if I was ever going to survive I would need the taste and desire for drugs to be taken away from me forever. I figured being sent to prison would help me curb the desire. Little did I know all the drugs I sold on the street could also be found illegally in the Texas prison where I would spend my time paying my debt to society.

As I sat day after day waiting to hear how much time I would receive, I often talked to my cellmates about the sentencing. Everyone was always interested in what punishment you received based on the crime you did. Finally my day for sentencing came, and soon I would be headed back to the court.

What I am about to tell you may sound very unusual, in fact it seemed bizarre to me at the time. As I was preparing for sentencing, it was as if God impressed upon my heart to make it known to all my cellmates I would be out in only four years. Now I did not hear an audible voice, and angels did not write this on the wall; I just knew it. It was written into my heart and mind.

When in court that day, the judge asked me to stand and read, "Jeremy Perry, for your crimes you will receive two thirty-year sentences running concurrently." My heart dropped. I thought God told me to tell everyone I would be out in four years. Now I was being sentenced to much longer. I felt betrayed until the same still, small voice impressed upon my heart the words, *Trust me.* It was as if God was telling me, *Make this known because I am going to do something to prove my power to you.* Yeah, I know, it sounded astonishing to me at the time, but I felt I had nothing to lose. Actually, I really believed it. I mean I saw a miracle occur before. I got to see my daughter being born, so why couldn't this happen also? I decided to trust God and follow what I believed he was telling me.

I went back to my cell after sentencing with a feeling of relief and trust in my heart. As soon as I went in, my cellmates started asking me how much time I got. Smiling I said, "Two thirty-year sentences." They looked at me, stunned, and asked, "Why are you smiling if you got two thirty-year sentences?" I said, "Because God told me I would be out in four." They thought I was crazy and began to make fun of me. I did not care—I knew what I knew and I believed God would have me out in four.

During this time my faith was strengthened, but my life became quite difficult. The other prisoners decided to make my life hell. I often heard about Christian persecution, but now I was experiencing it firsthand. I did not have to deal with it for too long because I was sent off to Coffield Prison in Texas. I landed in a big-time prison environment. This unit housed more than five thousand inmates. I can remember the first day I arrived at the facility; a helicopter was leaving the compound with an inmate who had been stabbed. Needless to say I was not looking forward to my new home.

I soon realized this prison had all the same corruption I got into on the outside. I could get drugs, alcohol, tobacco, and women here, all for the right price. This was like the drug-running operation I was in on the outside except gangs ran it on the inside. It was a bad place, and I was happy when I was transferred to Sanchez Unit in El Paso. It was there I met a thief, and together our lives took a whole new turn.

When a thief and a drug dealer get together, you would think it just can't be a good thing, and yet this is where our story takes an amazing turn. When Kyle and I met in a prison church service in December 2005, we were both in a better place emotionally in our lives. Sure, we were in prison, but we both really felt that our lives where changing for the better. After the service we struck up a conversation about any topic crossing our minds, then something remarkable happened.

He started telling me how he felt that God wanted him to start a Christian rap music group. The problem for Kyle was he hated rap music and thought he must be imagining things. This is where my ears began to perk up. I had also felt God moving me to do the same thing. I know you might be sitting there thinking, *These two guys are crazy*, and possibly we are, but neither of us could deny the strong impression we had to do this.

Kyle went back to his cell and grabbed his Bible; amazingly the songs and rhymes began to come so naturally. It was almost as if someone else was writing the words for him. I was having the same success on my end. It really felt like God was moving us to do something. Now I know a lot of people can imagine God is telling them to do something, but we not only believed it; we saw the results firsthand. If this was going to be a reality, lots of things would have to occur first. There were numerous obstacles to overcome, the main one being sentenced to long prison terms with mine of thirty years. Our only chance would be if we were granted an early parole.

Kyle was the first to come up for parole, and after his first meeting he was denied. We were both devastated. We now felt our dreams were starting to crash around us. I even thought maybe I imagined the whole direction from God. Thankfully, we were not ready to quit; so we prayed, waited, and kept the faith. Another eight months passed, and Kyle was once again up for parole. This time it was granted and he was released. It was a joyous day.

We talked ahead of time about his parole and where he would go once he got out. I told him he should head to Lubbock, Texas, and do his parole time at my mother's house. My mother had never met Kyle, and yet she was willing to take him in. (She really is an incredible woman.) Once I knew for sure Kyle would be released, I contacted my mom and made sure everything was good on her end. She was actually excited to be able to help someone out. So half of our music group would be on the outside getting ready to start the work God had for us.

Kyle and I felt God forgave us and he was giving us a second chance at life. It really brought me great peace of mind; but, realistically, if the courts, the justice system, and the people of America did not give us a second chance, what good would it do for us to ever get out. Now Kyle was on the outside and he would see firsthand if a second chance could be found among the American people.

Kyle began to make contacts with the right individuals. A youth pastor at a church took Kyle at his word and began to assist him with getting our music group set up. Sure we had no sophisticated music equipment, but it did not stop Kyle. He began recording songs through his computer with a mic and a set of headphones. The music flowed, and things began to take off. He was being offered a second chance; they accepted him for who he was now and not for who he once was. Kyle saw grace in action and it felt good.

Things were definitely going well except for one thing: I was still in prison and was due to serve thirty years. Yet, I still believed the promise God impressed on my heart—the promise I would only serve four years. Kyle was free for almost two years when I came up for my first parole. All the guys in prison laughed and made fun of my belief in this promise from God. I was on pins and needles. Would God keep his promise to me, or had I been imagining this the entire time? Would I be out of prison and on to a new life, or would I be still here? I had hope that I had not imagined this. The last thing I wanted to do was bring reproach and ridicule to the name of God.

The day came and I stood before the parole board. Each indictment was reviewed as was my service and conduct in prison. Then it happened. They told me I made parole. It had been four years, and I was going to be out. It was a miracle; God kept his word to me, and I could not wait to tell my cellmates. When they brought me back to my cell, I turned and told them all, "Good-bye, guys, I will see you later." Needless to say, they were shocked. For almost four years I told everyone about the promise God made to me. Now the power of God began to do a work inside this Texas state prison. I still believe God used my circumstances to magnify the fact he is still involved in the lives of everyday people.

My grandmother had always told me God gave people second chances. I now know he gives third and fourth chances also. Many people around the world know nothing of freedom, let alone the gift of a second chance. When those persecuted souls boarded the Mayflower, they wanted another chance, a place where they could start life anew. John Adams said on July 1, 1776, "Set before the people the object of entire independence and it will breathe into them anew the spirit of life." I was now free to pursue a new life.

We certainly did not deserve a second chance, but we both knew if we received one, that we would do everything in our power to right the wrongs we committed. The pilgrims were treated as criminals; we on the other hand were criminals. They did nothing wrong but serve God, yet we had done everything wrong. With a second chance, however, we would now wholeheartedly serve him. They placed their lives in the hand of Providence, trusting he would sustain them. I knew we must do the very same thing.

After I returned home we started our music group, Soldiers of God. We travel America warning people of the error of actions. We have been privileged to sing and speak to thousands of people all over the United States. Had we been anywhere else in the world, Kyle and I would probably never have had the chance to start over. A new chapter in our lives is being written, however, because God and the people of America chose to show us

grace.

THROUGH THE
Perilous
Fight

I fired several shots, sending bullets tearing through a living, breathing human. He dropped to his knees, gasping for any vestige of life, but it was to no avail. Crashing to the ground, his last signs of life disappeared. In the middle of it all I felt no sorrow or grief. My mind convinced me he was not really a person, that he had no humanity. Over the years my feelings would change; nevertheless, I was still tortured by the memories, and I wondered if I would ever find peace. My country made me a hero, but my conscience told me I was a criminal.

My name is Woody. This is my story of America.

★ ★ ★

My life started normally for someone growing up on a dairy farm in the 1920s. My mother and father were blessed with eleven children, and all of us were required to work around the farm to keep things going. Our days began at the crack of dawn—the time when the sun is just starting to rise from its nightly slumber. Brisk, cool mountain air filled the morning skies as we made our way to the barn and chicken coop. Fresh eggs were collected, and the task of milking cows began. Making butter by hand was a backbreaking daily task. This was my existence, but it was the only life I knew, so I just accepted it.

The morning tasks never seemed to be completed before the time came for loading Dad's Model A Ford with fresh bottles of milk; thus began our days of deliveries.

With no refrigeration available, milk had to be delivered daily. Our truck rumbled up and down the dirt roads of our rural community with the clanking of the glass bottles sending notification—the milkman is coming. Every day I marched up to doors with full bottles in hand and returned with empty ones. Seven days a week, all year long, the cycle repeated.

Growing up I learned a lot about births—the birth of animals and the birth of children. Because we had no hospital in the area, my mother and our neighbor Myrtle took turns serving as midwife for each other. When Myrtle's pregnancies came to term, my mom went over there and delivered the baby. Then when it was my mom's turn, Myrtle arrived to return the favor.

My mom had eleven kids and Myrtle had thirteen— you might say they were quite experienced at their part-time profession.

Not only did I know a lot about births; I soon learned a lot about death. This unfortunate part of life surrounded me far too often. In one year's time the flu claimed the lives of six of my siblings. This terrible sickness swept through our community, killing several and devastating everyone.

Then at the tender age of nine I lost my dad. A heart condition took away my role model and best friend; a young boy should never have to experience such a tragedy. It left my five-foot-two-inch mother all alone, trying to raise a family and run a dairy farm. The difficulties were enormous, but we banded together and survived. My oldest brother stepped up and took on the responsibility of managing the farm. He hired the rest of us as farmhands, for no pay of course.

The community where we lived had no church or courthouse. The only record of family births or deaths was kept in the large family Bible on our coffee table. We really never used it for any other purpose but to record those facts. Actually, I had never been in a church, but I did visit the outside of one particular house of worship every Sunday.

Growing up in a rural community in West Virginia can have its disadvantages in many ways. In our community, the boys outnumbered the girls by a considerable margin. To remedy this situation I developed a full-proof plan. Every Sunday my brothers and I walked several miles over into the next community. We waited outside a little country church for service to be over. I had no interest in what was going on inside, but I sure was fascinated by who came out of the church once the service was over: girls!

That church was filled with pretty girls. I can remember doing everything I could to convince one of them to let me walk her home. Yes sir, I was a regular churchgoer—well, at least in the summer months. This was strictly a fair-weather activity, and come winter, my pursuits of love were put on the shelf. By the first signs of spring, I was ready to pursue my heart's desire all over again. "Any girl is a pretty girl," was my motto.

I can remember standing outside the door of the church talking with my brothers. Nothing important came up; we just talked about the girls. I loved going to church, or at least to the church. Meeting girls this way was a great idea to me, but it was a terrible idea with the boys who lived there. They did not like us coming into their community trying to steal their girls every Sunday. Those boys exited the church with a chip on their shoulder. The love of God soon disappeared from their mind when the first punches were landed.

Bloody noses soon started flowing, closely followed with rocks being thrown. It was certainly no display of brotherly love or Christian fellowship. With the many Sundays I went home empty handed, you might think I would have been discouraged. Nonetheless it only took one instance of winning the fight and securing the girl to make it all worthwhile.

I had no idea at the time fighting would become such an integral part of my future. The battles of my youth would be displaced by a much larger war—a war started with my body but fought later with my mind. I was not prepared to engage this conflict.

While I was growing up I never really had any spending money. All of the family basically just worked to survive so we could keep food on the table. My brother closest in age to me never liked farming so when he was sixteen he joined the Civilian Conservation Corps (CCC). This was a public works relief program that provided unskilled manual labor jobs related to the conservation and development of natural resources in rural lands.

My brother was sent to a small community about fifty miles from where we lived. He made twenty-one dollars a month. When he came home I thought he was rich, so I was determined to make big money just like my brother. Seeing his newfound wealth encouraged me to follow his chosen path in life.

Before I knew it, I was signed up for the CCC. In my mind I would be headed to work alongside my brother. I naively thought there was only one CCC camp, and of course I believed it was in our state. I was so wrong.

First I was sent to a camp north of where we lived, some ninety miles from my brother. After working there a few months, they decided my talents would be better utilized two thousand miles across country. Montana, here I come.

I wasn't there long when the fateful "date that will live in infamy" occurred; the Japanese bombed our naval base at Pearl Harbor. To be honest, it did not mean anything to me. I had no clue there was a Hawaii, let alone a Pearl Harbor. Most of us guys in the camp never heard of the Japanese and had never seen any.

The day after it occurred our leaders called all of us outside where we were ordered to fall into formation. Two hundred sixty-five of us stood there wondering what was going on. My body grew tense and goose bumps ran down my arms like they were running a race when they delivered the news: "Americans had been attacked and killed. Our naval base at Pearl Harbor, Hawaii, had been destroyed. We are going to war!"

Those words echoed repeatedly through my mind as they presented options to us. We could go straight into the army, or we could get our release and return home. Once we arrived home we could then enlist with the military service branch of our choice. America needed us, and each one of us there chose to do our part to defend our freedom.

The choice for me was real easy. I would return home so I could enlist in the Marine Corps. Where I lived growing up, I was influenced by a couple of people who were Marines. I can remember in particular one of those guys. He got one thirty-day furlough a year, and the Marines required him to wear his uniform the entire time. The Corps was trying to make its name well known, so to help with recruiting they always required their men to be in their dress blues throughout the community. You can only imagine the attention he commanded walking around our little rural area in his fancy blue uniform. Well, their marketing campaign worked. Yes sir, the Marines was the place for me.

When I returned from the CCC, I immediately told my mother I wanted to enlist. She had none of it. I was only seventeen at the time so I needed her permission to enter the Corps. No amount of begging persuaded her. I decided to just wait out the last few months until I turned eighteen.

In those days when you turned eighteen, people looked at you as if you were a man. In fact, you were expected to accept responsibility for yourself and make a transformation from childhood into adulthood. I personally was ready to make this move and get on with my life.

So my eighteenth birthday came in October, and by November I was headed to the enlistment station to become a Marine. I was excited and figured nothing could stop me now; boy, was I wrong. The Marine Corps had a height requirement, and I was too short. They required a recruit to be at least five feet eight inches tall. I unfortunately fell two inches shy. Nothing I could do would help me grow those last two inches. When they told me the news, I was so dejected. Reluctantly I returned home to the farm, relegated to a life I no longer desired.

To my good fortune, by 1943 the war was starting to build up, and the Marines desperately needed men. They lowered the height requirement to anyone above five feet tall. Bingo, I could now join the Corps and serve my country. Before I knew it I was headed to California for basic training.

I had never heard of this place called San Diego, but I was about to be formally introduced to Camp Pendleton. I always thought I was prepared for any situation, but this was definitely a new experience on me. This was no life on the farm.

It is rather funny to think how I was so naïve about the military and the job we would be doing. In my mind, we would stay in America and protect her by guarding the border. We were going to gather around this country anywhere we were needed, daring the enemy to come and try to overtake it. This was not at all what the Marine Corps had in mind. I soon learned we would be going to the Pacific to take back islands from the Japanese. *Where is this Pacific they keep talking about?*

For the next several months, I was instructed in how to protect myself and how to kill. As a boy on a farm, we were taught never to kill anything unless it was for food or to put an animal out of its misery. The most dangerous weapon I ever used was a slingshot or a BB gun.

I recall one summer day I sat on a fence with my slingshot in hand. Rocks filled my pocket as bullets line a gun belt. Hitting inanimate objects had grown dull. I wanted a greater challenge. I scanned the area, and an opportunity presented to me my next target. A small bird landed on the fencepost only a short distance from me. I was determined to hit the bull's-eye.

Slowly I reached into my pocket, feeling around for the perfect piece of ammunition. I eased the stone into the strap of my weapon, raising my arms as I took dead aim. Quietly I pulled back the strap, watching my prey move slightly from side to side on the post. With the bird clearly in my sights, I let the rock fly. *Whack*, a perfect shot. Feathers scattered as the bird dropped to the ground. I took its life for the joy of killing, yet it brought no joy, only remorse. My remorse turned to pain later as my father gave me a whipping for killing the bird. I was instructed you just do not kill unless there was a darn good reason.

His instruction flooded my adult mind as I learned through my military training that I would not be killing animals. Instead, I would be killing humans—real, living, breathing people whom I never met and whom never did anything to me personally. The Japanese were now my enemy. My job was to hasten their death. Killing the small bird tormented me for quite some time, but ending the life of a person was a torture for which my mind was not prepared.

My first stop in the war was the island of Guadalcanal. We went there for training to prepare ourselves for the attack on the island of Bougainville. It was where the Marines were fighting and where I saw my first military combat. As Marines we were trained to be riflemen first of all, so if we were needed to be on the front lines we were prepared.

While I was on Guadalcanal, officers decided to form a special weapons unit consisting of flamethrowers. We did not have flamethrowers before so this was all new to me. I was trained on how to use the weapon and cross-trained as a demolition man. This cross-training turned out to be quite valuable. In fact, my life was changed because of it.

In war, plans can often deviate and it was no different for us. Originally we were scheduled to go to Bougainville; instead we ended up in Guam. We were told the Japanese killed everyone on the island, and it was our territory. Our job would be to take it back, securing it for our use.

This task proved to be a difficult one because of the jungle environment and the ability of the Japanese to disappear in the heavy brush. It was not uncommon for a Japanese soldier to have himself tied to a branch up in a tree and fire upon us as we walked below.

The time came; we circled the island to find a suitable place for a beach landing. It would be my first taste of combat, my first taste of killing.

As soon as we landed on the beach, the Japanese immediately fired upon us. Directly in front of me was a huge hill just off the beach. My focus turned to the apex of the hill where Japanese soldiers controlled the high ground. Mercilessly they rained bullets down upon us.

If we were going to be successful, we had to overrun their position. This would prove to be an enormous challenge. As I made my way to the base of the hill, I realized it was so steep there was no way I could walk up it. I got down on my knees then dropped to my stomach and began crawling up this mountain.

For the next five days I, as well as my fellow Marines, attempted to crawl up this hill. Every time we made some progress, the Japanese killed a group of us. Hand grenades rolled from the top of the hill, exploding all around me. Mortars rained down like hail. Friend and fellow soldiers were dying as I made my way closer to the top.

On the fourth day, as I crawled along with my rifle in my hands, I felt as if I was advancing only inches at a time. A mortar exploded nearby, and I noticed a helmet lying on the hillside with the opening pointed to the sky. No one else was near, so I glanced into the helmet and saw some bundled letters. I assumed they were letters from home, and I stuffed them in my pack for protection. (How precious letters like these are to men in combat!) I knew if I lived I would have to get these letters back to their owner.

Finally, on the fifth day we got to the top of the ridge. Immediately we began to dig foxholes for protection. We set up an outpost in front of the line stationed near the edge of the hill. Two Marines were placed in the foxhole to warn us if the Japanese were advancing.

I was chosen to be one of those Marines, and I was the BAR man, which stood for Browning automatic rifle. For several days I sat there protecting our position until I traded places with Clevenger, who was a good friend of mine.

They moved me to another part of the hill while he took over my post and ran the BAR. Things were quiet for a few days as we had the advantage, but then it happened. The Japanese overran our position, and Clevenger as well as another soldier were killed trying to protect us. They broke through our lines, killing a bunch of us as they made their way to the rear of our unit where our supply team and medical staff were located. Several of those guys lost their lives as well.

It occurred to me, had I not traded positions with Clevenger I would be dead. It was the first time I comprehended how he died in my place. This was not a game; these were real people dying, and death became so real to me. It was one thing to see people you don't know die, but it was something totally different to watch your friends perish. It was devastating, and it was happening daily.

As we made our way through the jungle, we often had to use a machete to hack through the brush. We could not even see the enemy as we fired our shots because the jungle was so thick. Sometimes we just fired into the area where the shots were coming from. Then we went through after the battle was over. I saw dead bodies lying on the jungle floor and wondered how many I killed. I did not know the answer; I only knew the jungle floor was littered with dead people and I was partly responsible.

Many a Marine began to fight the same battle I was: the battle against your mind. Some literally had nervous break-downs on the battlefield and had to be evacuated. On more than one occasion my fellow soldiers said to me, "I am not going to make it. I am never going to get back home." I just knew I could not permit myself to contemplate these thoughts. The only way I, or any of us, could survive was to view the enemy as non-persons—they were only things that had to be eliminated. It was a difficult separation. Unfortunately, many soldiers lost this battle with their mind, and for a long time it seemed I would also be a casualty.

After we secured the island of Guam, I remembered the letters I found and took them out of my pack. The return address was listed on the envelopes so I had them sent there. I did not know whose letters they were, but I figured the person who wrote them would know. Sure enough some weeks later a soldier by the name of Lefty Lee tracked me down and thanked me for sending the letters home. He was wounded in the first battle we experienced on Guam and was shipped back to Hawaii for treatment. He returned for more action, and he just wanted to make sure I knew he appreciated what I did. As I said, letters from home were like gold to us.

After the Guam campaign we boarded a ship and headed to the island of Iwo Jima. An officer told us we would be gone about five days. Most likely we would never get off the ship. We were going to be a reserve unit used strictly for back up. At the time, the Marine Corps had no idea the Japanese had twenty-one thousand troops on the island. Iwo Jima is only five miles long by two-and-a-half miles wide, and the thought of so many Japanese troops occupying such a tiny place seemed illogical. Yet, they built an intricate network of tunnels. End to end, those tunnels measured more than nineteen miles. To say they were well hidden is a major understatement.

> *I regret I have but one life to lose for my country.*
>
> — NATHAN HALE

On previous missions when we attacked an island, the Japanese fired on us before we could place boots on the sand. On those occasions they did not want us to set one foot on the island. Iwo Jima would be very different.

The commanding officer of this Japanese unit wanted the Marines to land on the beach. For as soon as they did, Japanese soldiers came from everywhere and overwhelmed them. You could not throw a rock anywhere without hitting a Japanese soldier. They came from underground, pouring from tunnels dug into the sides of the hill.

The Marines who first landed on Iwo Jima did not know what hit them; the enemy was suddenly everywhere. There were so many casualties on the first day we could not count them all. It was quickly clear to me we would have to go in; we would definitely be getting off the boat and hitting the island.

On February 20, 1945, we got into our Higgins boats and began to circle the island, looking for a place to land. The beach was carpeted with dead Marines and Japanese soldiers. Everywhere we tried had no area for landing.

On the next day we tried again and found an opening. The magnitude of the situation as I exited the boat cannot be described.

As soon as we hit the beach, we started losing people. Six individuals made up my special weapons unit. I was tasked with supplying them with whatever they needed to fight the battle. At the same time I was firing my rifle at the enemy, just trying to stay alive. Unfortunately, by the twenty-third all six of my team were dead or wounded; I alone remained.

While some of our other Marines were having success with their battle and raising the flag on Mount Suribachi, we were having difficulty in ours. In front of us was a series of reinforced concrete bunkers with walls some two feet thick. We called them pillboxes. These pillboxes had roofs and small doors in the back. After entry, a Japanese officer some-times locked the door behind him. They were told by their commanding officer they would never leave the island; this is where they would die. But before they did, they were to take ten Marines with them. To surrender was a disgrace for a Japanese soldier. They would die before they would surrender.

These pillboxes stood between us and where we needed to go. The problem we faced was enormous. They held all the fields of fire. It was impossible for us to get by one of those pillboxes without being seen by the next one in line. We battled all day long and took an immense number of casualties. We were taking casualties in bucket loads. There were only two officers remaining, and all of my immediate commanding officers were killed. It was truly a desperate situation.

One of the officers called a meeting of all the NCOs (non-commissioned officers). I was a corporal, and because I was in charge of a unit, he told me to go to this meeting. Normally I would not have attended because I was just a corporal, but these were extenuating circumstances. We all got together in a shell crater where we could be protected from some of the grazing fire. The commanding officer was looking for ideas from anyone who could figure a way past this string of pill-boxes. He turned and asked me if I could do anything with the flamethrower. To be honest with you, I have no clue what my answer was, but some of the men said I told him, "I would try."

After a moment of planning, I was assigned four Marines to provide cover. One of those Marines was Lefty Lee.

A flamethrower weighed some seventy pounds, containing about four-and-a-half gallons of gasoline and diesel fuel mixed. If you fired the flamethrower without ceasing, it would last only seventy-two seconds, so we were taught to shoot in two- or three-second bursts. Instead of shooting it into the air, we were trained to shoot it on the ground and roll it into a cave or pillbox. The forced air I carried along with the equipment would take the flame about ten or fifteen yards.

I hate to admit this, but as I got started I really had no clue what I was going to do. I just knew I was going to try and burn out pillboxes. As we made our way to target number one, I placed two Marines on one side of me and two on the other side so they could crossfire upon the first pillbox. I was quite vulnerable carrying this seventy-pound flamethrower; but I was placing my life into the hands of my fellow Marines, and I knew they would protect me.

I heard them open fire as I made my way toward the target. As I reached the front I steadied my weapon and pulled the trigger. A large ball of fire shot directly into the interior of the first pillbox. Screams of terror and death came rolling from within. I could now smell the stench of burnt flesh, and it was something I would never get out of my mind or senses. Over the next four hours my memory would escape me for much of the time. I attribute this to fear.

The Japanese dug trenches into the ground between the pillboxes. This allowed them to crawl out from beneath one unit unseen and make their way to another. This was a very effective technique.

After I knocked out the first pillbox, I was crawling along in one of these trenches when I heard the sound of bullets ricocheting off the flamethrower strapped to my back. I managed to avoid being shot and got up to the side of the pillbox from where the shots were coming. Immediately I shot forth another burst of fire and killed all the inhabitants. The death toll of Japanese soldiers attributed to me was climbing. Those facts did not matter to me. This was a battle to survive.

The next unit I came upon seemed to have a small vent pipe sticking up out of the top of it. The Japanese practically lived in these bunkers, so they needed a way to vent smoke from cooking or the exhaust from their weaponry.

They were firing their weapons at us relentlessly as I made my way toward the back of their bunker. I heard a scream behind me as one of my cover men was shot and killed. I was now more determined than ever to seek revenge. As I reached the back, I climbed up on top and stuck my flamethrower down the vent pipe and pulled the trigger. Seventeen Japanese soldiers quickly expired.

I have often been told how brave I was, and it might be so, but the fear of the situation drove me more than any bravery I might have felt. It was instinct; it was either them or me. You do not think about the killing. It is just something you must do to stay alive.

I approached the next pillbox, trying to get to the front of it so I could shoot flame inside. The enemy in this unit had apparently run out of ammunition so they came out of the back door with bayonets attached to their rifles. They charged straight toward me. It was almost as if everything was happening in slow motion. I had fuel left in the tank so I pulled the trigger, and a ball of flame engulfed their bodies. Screaming in agony, they dropped to the ground as their lives ended.

Over the course of the next four hours I was able to take out seven of those pillboxes with six flamethrowers. I had no idea where I got the strength and stamina; I only remember praying to God to let me live. Each time my weapon ran out of fuel I lay it down and headed back to the storage area to retrieve another unit.

I used to say the Marines providing my cover did not like me much because none of them ever volunteered to walk back to get a new flamethrower for me. Actually, nothing could be farther from the truth because two of those Marines gave their lives for me. This was the second time in battle someone had died in my place. Thankfully this fact never left me and later provided my escape from the hellhole my mind became.

The Japanese built quite an impressive array of tunnels and caves on the island; they most certainly used them to their military advantage. They had one cave set up to roll armament out the front so they could fire toward the ocean. As soon as the weapon was discharged, it was immediately rolled back in so you could not see from where the shot came. This cave became my next battleground.

My commanding officer approached me about this mission. He said three hundred Japanese soldiers were inside. My assignment was to blow up the entrance and seal them in. Because I had already been doing some demolition work on the island, I figured this task wouldn't be very difficult.

I always carried two satchels of composition C2 explosives on my shoulders in addition to my rifle. Composition C2 came in one-pound blocks, and I carried eight in one bag. They stationed a couple of guys on each side of the cave in case the enemy came out after me while I was approaching the opening.

In the top of my pack I carried a box of blasting caps that were absolutely essential because without them the explosive would not work. The situation was beyond tense as I slowly crawled toward the front of the cave. I was in an extremely vulnerable position, and my hands shook as I took one of my satchel charges off my shoulder. I prepared the charge and fastened a ten-second fuse to it. I figured this would be enough time for me to throw my eight-pound bag into the entrance and get out of the way.

Dropping to my stomach I got as low to the ground as I could and began to crawl the rest of the way to the cave. With the fuse now prepared, I quickly set fire to it, stood up, and threw the bag of explosives into the cave.

Like a shot from a cannon I took off running from the entrance and dove into the sand. I heard the cap go off but no explosion. I had failed. I was never raised to be a failure, and I was not going to start then. I began the process all over again.

I took the second satchel from my shoulder and went through the same routine as before. I lit the fuse, stood up, and hurled the bag of C2 into the cave entrance; for the second time I ran like a wild man in the opposite direction and dove into the sand covering my head. *Plop*, no explosion. It suddenly occurred to me what the problem was. My blasting caps had drawn some dampness so they were not going to detonate.

Frustrated, I walked back to my supply group and got some new blasting caps as well as two more satchels of C2. Unfazed by the previous failures, I was determined to accomplish my mission.

For the third time I crawled up to the cave entrance. I took the bag of explosives, just as I had the other two, lit the fuse, and threw it into the cave. When I threw this bag I had no clue where the other bags had landed, but this one landed right between them. I took off running, dove into the sand, and this time the blasting caps detonated. The explosion was so massive you could not tell a cave had even been there. Rocks rained down from the sky and the earth shook. The cave was now permanently sealed shut, and nothing or no one would ever get out.

We were never quite sure how many Japanese were in the cave, but I was told I buried three hundred of them alive, sealing their fate. Sometimes it's the unknown that gives you fits, and my memory tortured my mind with the re-occurrence of this event.

I spent a total of thirty-four days on the island of Iwo Jima; from there I went back to Guam. I was preparing to go to my next field of combat when the bombs were dropped on Nagasaki and Hiroshima. My days of fighting the Japanese abruptly ended; however, my mental war was just beginning.

I received notification I was to be called back to the United States to receive the Medal of Honor. I had never even heard of such an award. In fact, those words had never been voiced anywhere I could of heard them. I did not comprehend what I did as being such a big deal. I was doing only what I was supposed to do.

When I returned to the states I was told I would soon be meeting with the general; this was not something that made me feel very good. It was just not common for a corporal to meet with a general, so I felt rather uneasy about it. He explained to me how I was going to receive the Medal of Honor. It really did not mean much to me at the time.

I was flown to Washington on the third of October, then on October 5, 1945, the Medal of Honor was presented to me. I still did not understand why I was selected; two of the Marines who were giving me protection died in the process. *Why me?* kept going through my mind; they gave their lives and I didn't. I truly believe they should have received the award.

The day after I was given the medal, I was called into the commandant's office. Again, this interaction was quite unusual, and I remember I was more frightened to talk to him than I was talking to the president. I did not know at the time, but the commandant was also a Medal of Honor recipient. So as I walked into his office he turned to greet me, then he spoke the words I will never forget.

"The medal you received yesterday does not belong to you." I was shocked by his words, and my body froze as thoughts began to race through my mind, *How could this be? I just got it yesterday.* It was the only thing I could keep thinking. Then after a brief pause he continued and said, "It belongs to all the Marines who never got to come home. Make sure you always remember that."

On that day my life really changed, and from that time forward I have always worn the medal in memory of those Marines who did not come home, especially for the two who gave their lives for me on Iwo Jima. They sacrificed their lives so I could live. I am alive because they died for me. It is a fact that completely overwhelms me.

In 1945 I had the opportunity to re-enlist or leave the Marine Corps. Because I had a girl back home who agreed to be my fiancée, I decided to leave the service so I could be married. I always wanted to have a wife and start a family. Ruby and I had been engaged since 1943. We survived the test of time and my battles of war.

When I finally arrived home, Ruby was so excited to see me. I thought of her every day I was away. That was actually quite easy—not only was I in love with her, but she gave me a ruby ring to remember her by. She purchased it from the G. C. Murphy five- and ten-cent store before I left. She told me, "Woody, this is a ruby ring, so you look at it and remember me." I had no clue the stone was really called a ruby; I just thought she named the ring Ruby.

When I went to war I had an assistant by the name of Vernon from Floyd, Montana, a mountain of a man standing six feet six inches tall. One night in our tent we were talking about our homes when he showed me the ring his father gave him. In return I showed him the ring from Ruby. We decided if anything ever happened to either of us we would make sure to get the ring back to the giver.

We shook hands on it, not knowing at the time that if you removed any personal item from a Marine after death it could lead to a court martial. It would have made no difference in our minds anyway. Our word was our bond.

The battle on Iwo Jima reduced my company's strength from 278 to 17. The Japanese killed many with mortar rounds. They had a little weapon called the knee mortar. This unit was only about twenty-four inches high, and they strapped it to their knee to fire. Once, while trying to avoid being hit, I dove to a low place in the ground. I managed to get most of my body into it except my lower body. Unfortunately, a mortar landed nearby, and a piece of metal went into my leg. The burning pain was excruciating.

I called for a corpsman to come over. He cut a hole in my trousers and extracted the shrapnel. He dusted the wound with sulfur powder and applied a bandage. He pulled a tag out of his coat and placed it on me saying, "You have to go back." I informed him, "I am not going back. I am going forward to fight." Angrily he said, "I have tagged you so you have to go back; it is the rule." I reached over, tore the tag off, and said, "I have no tag now." He left shouting, "If you are that stupid then just forget it!"

I made my way back toward the battlefield as Vernon came running past me. He did not get far before he took a direct hit from a mortar to the head. I froze as I watched him fall to the ground, then I quickly crawled over to him and realized he was dead. There was only one thing I could do for him: get his ring back home to his dad. I reached down, grabbed his finger, and worked feverishly to get that ring off, but it was stuck. Hastily I spit on his hand, managing to loosen the ring and get it off. Beneath it his finger was extremely white so I knew someone would notice the ring was gone. I rubbed together a mixture of sand and dirt on the area of the finger, turning it dark like the rest of his hand.

I knew it was the right thing to do because I made a promise to Vernon to get his ring back to his father. I intended to keep my word, so I stuck the ring in my pocket and went on. When I got back to Guam after the battle at Iwo Jima, I wrote to his folks and told them I had the ring, but I was not going to put it in the mail out of fear someone would take it. I promised them I would deliver it in person when I got home. I was sure I would be coming back. I did not know God or even whether he existed, but somehow I knew he would make sure I could keep my word.

I got out of the service in November 1945, and in January of 1946 I decided it was time for me to make the trip to Montana so I could deliver Vernon's ring. There was just one problem: I had no car, no money, and no idea how I was going to get to Montana.

A fellow who had taken a liking to me had a car dealership so he let me use an old 1942 red Dodge convertible to make the trip. Ruby and I packed and headed west. It took us three days to get there, and on more than one occasion we had car trouble. When we delivered Vernon's ring to his father, you would have thought we were bringing him the most precious thing in the world. As he cried I could not help but think how this man's son died so others might live.

For the next several years, my life was quite different. I was married to a wonderful woman, Ruby, and we had two beautiful girls. My wife was a good woman, a Christian, and a great mother. There was nothing more I could want in life except for perhaps a new mind.

I never really knew how many men I killed. There were guys I went to battle with who came back with a mental breakdown, and I was determined I was not going to let that happen to me. However, I felt as if I was beginning to lose the battle. I so wanted peace but had no clue how to find it.

Killing people you did not know was distressing, but watching people you had come to know and even love die right in front of you was utterly devastating. I was able to deal with it partially because I received the Medal of Honor, and I talked to people about what happened on the island of Iwo Jima. Yet, I still had no peace. I was living in the "Land of the Free and the Home of the Brave," but it was not the place of peace I knew when I was a kid.

Easter of 1962 came around, and once again the full-court press was put on me to attend church with my wife and children. I always had a great excuse not to go. The car needed washing, or the bathroom, which didn't really need painting, now needed another coat of paint. I had the master playbook of church excuses. I understood there had to be a Creator who brought me into this world. I also knew I asked him to protect me during the war and he did. Other than this I did not acknowledge him, nor did I want to recognize him. The only thing I knew I wanted was to find relief from the grand tormentor of my mind.

So on Easter morning, my two little angels walked in with their beautiful dresses and looked up at me with adoring eyes and asked, "Daddy, will you please go to church with us?" I fought in war and survived many conflicts, but this was a battle I would lose, so I unwillingly surrendered. Today I would go to church with my little girls.

As we entered the building I began to scope out a place where I could make a quick exit if necessary. We sat about five rows back from the front, and I made sure to sit on the aisle; from here I could easily make an escape should the heat get too hot. Like my dead friend Vernon, the preacher was a big man. As soon as he began to speak, I immediately felt alone. It was as if no one was in the building but me. In fact, it seemed as if he was staring straight into my eyes. Even when he was looking the other way, he was still staring in my direction.

He began to tell the story of the Son of God who left the beauty of heaven to die for the sins of all mankind. As he told the story of the death of Christ on the cross, he began to pound his left fist into his right hand to imitate the sound of the hammer driving the nails through the hands of Jesus. Each pound he made drove a stake through my heart. He then delivered what would be the final blow. He looked at me and said, "The Father gave his Son, so that you might live. Jesus willingly gave his life so you could live. Together they did this so you could find absolute peace and complete forgiveness."

My memories all came flooding to the surface. I thought of the men who willingly gave their lives for me at Iwo Jima. I thought about Vernon's dad giving up his son so I could live. For so long I never had peace or forgiveness, now it seemed to be right before me.

I could not take this full frontal assault any longer. I hastily got up out of the pew and stepped out to leave, except I did not turn to the door. Instead, I slowly went forward and stood before the large preacher. He stopped midsentence, looked down at me from the stage, and said "Can I help you sir?" I looked up at him and said, "I need that, I need that peace and forgiveness. Can you please help me?"

From 1775 men have been dying in this country so we could have peace. In fact, our nation declared independence to have freedom to worship, and some 187 years later I was still reaping the rewards of their sacrifice. Because of this fact I walked out of the church with something I did not have since I went to war. I once again had peace; I knew I was now

 *forgiven!*

O'ER THE
Ramparts
We Watched

I slowly opened the tube of toothpaste, and hidden inside was the money my father managed to smuggle out of the country. The soldiers thoroughly checked everything over, but his ingenuity managed to get past their detection. Many people would love the thought of running off to an island paradise to live. Unfortunately our life depended on our ability to flee from one.

My name is Ana. This is my story of America.

If you are anything at all like me, your family is very important to you. My mother, my father, and my siblings mean the world to me. Looking back over my life, I can say, confidently, I have been truly blessed. If my father were still alive, he would definitely agree even though we almost lost our family when the Communist regime of Fidel Castro came to power in our home country of Cuba.

Growing up on an island in the Caribbean was quite magical for me. We did not have much money, but that did not matter. Material wealth never brings happiness, but the contentment you receive from spending time with those you love is limitless. Faith, family, and friends formed the foundation of our home.

My daddy was a hard worker and incredibly smart. Not only did he have a master's in agriculture; he was also a teacher by trade with three PhDs. All his students loved him because he made things so easy to understand. It was because of this talent and expertise he was made a target by the Castro regime.

Growing up in Cuba was absolutely incredible. I had a very nice childhood, and because my father loved agriculture, our yard was filled with fruit trees. I can remember coming home from school and climbing those trees, picking fruit for my afternoon snack. The variety seemed limitless to me. As soon as the school bell rang, I raced home to sample the tropical pleasures awaiting me at the end of those branches.

The soil on the island was so rich you could grow anything in it. I can remember on one occasion my father went to the schoolyard and took some branches from one of the ambarella trees, which produces tropical fruit similar to a plum. He brought them home and planted them. Within a few years we had this awesome fruit available to us in our own backyard. The dirt was so rich you could get a yield of three crops a year. Because of the climate and good growing conditions, no one ever went hungry.

We grew so much of our own food. It was absolutely wonderful to come into our home and smell the delicious aromas coming from our stove. My mother was such a great cook we always had extra people at the table. Food, family, and friends are a perfect mix, and all three surrounded my life.

My father taught at a private school on the island run by the Presbyterian church. The education they provided was second to none. In fact, we were required to attend a fifth year of high school to ensure we were properly prepared to enter the world and become a success. For the most part, the education system in Cuba was pretty good, even in the public arena. Our school focused heavily on the core subjects as well as world history and geography.

From my early childhood through my teenage years, my world was happy and carefree. We went anywhere we wanted on the island. The white sandy beaches pressed against clear blue water paint a picture so serene one finds it difficult to even imagine a better sight. Yes, I grew up on an island paradise, and I assumed I would never leave. Yet all of that changed the day the Communist revolution overtook Cuba.

Being so young at the time, I did not know a lot about the leader of our country. Fungencio Batista was president of Cuba from 1940 to 1944, then he became dictator from 1952 to 1959. Like many leaders, power went to his head, and he started taking advantage of the people. Anyone who spoke out against him usually ended up in a bad state of circumstances. Most of the time a beating from his hired thugs was enough to keep people in line.

Even though it was not the best situation for us, we still had a great deal of freedom and the country was prospering. It did not feel like we lived in a dictatorship. Yet, because of the corruption of his government and the misuse of funds, people became restless, and they were primed to be taken in by something worse.

You would think we learned something from history, but people seem to always repeat the same mistakes. They never learn from the failures of others. Adolph Hitler gained popularity by playing on the sympathies of the poor and downtrodden of his day. He manipulated their needs and desires so he could build his Nazi Party. Fidel Castro was no different.

Castro began his revolution by appealing to the poor workers on the island. They were being treated unfairly, and he would fight for them. Fidel came in promising democracy and freedom, but what he really brought was slavery and destruction. When Castro and his rebels marched into Havana in 1959, they were welcomed as conquering heroes by the cheering crowds. Those people had no way of knowing this revolution would soon rob them of their most basic human rights and political freedoms.

The year before the revolution began I went to the United States to attend college. I was unaware of what was happening in my homeland, but once I was made aware, I immediately began to worry for my family. The stories I was told sent chills down my spine. My homeland would no longer be the place I always knew and loved. It was headed to a disastrous destination.

All over the country people were losing their homes, farms, and valuables to the newly installed Communist government. Just down the road from where my father was born there was a beautiful farm. The owner had large palm trees all over his property. Those trees produced some of the best fruit in the area, which he fed to his herd of pigs. The farmer was known far and wide as having the best meat you could purchase any-where. We all believed it was because of the way he cared for those pigs. He fed them like kings.

Unfortunately, Fidel decided the government needed his land. They came in and cut down all the trees, destroyed the animals, and left the poor farmer with nothing. It was not un-common for Castro's Communist cronies to come take a per-son's home and give it to someone else. Often they would put several families in one residence and tell them this is where they must live. Freedom was gone, and the Cubans who cheered for revolution were left crying in the streets.

As the people became poorer, Fidel and his family became richer. His government thrived while average Cubans died. My years of study in world history taught me this is what always occurs with Communism. People are told they will be taken care of, and then the government leaves them out in the cold. Maybe this is why the United States motto says, "In God we trust," because "in government we trust" never quite works.

Fidel was not alone when it came to his totalitarian ideas. Sure he was fully backed by the Soviet Union, but he also had some cold-blooded assassins assisting him with his reign of terror.

Che Guevara was one of these men. He was a mainstay of the hard-line pro-Soviet faction presiding over the Cuban Revolution's first firing squads. He founded Cuba's "labor camp" system, which was nothing more than a place to incar-cerate your enemies or those who disagreed with your godless principles.

In front of the Havana Harbor stood two castles. Parts of them were strategically placed over the water so a trap door could be opened from the inside. Any person standing on that door dropped into the shark-infested waters below. The firing squads executed the dissenters, and their bodies were dropped through these doors, never to be seen again. An untold number of people were killed.

This was our new government. Remember, the one who was going to help the poor and needy. Everyone was clamoring for hope and change, but what we received was not what anyone would ever have wanted.

Che Guevara liked to proclaim himself a modern-day Robin Hood, when in fact he was nothing but a cowardly butcher who robbed from all. It is quite disturbing to see people today walking around with his picture on T-shirts proclaiming what a great freedom fighter he was. Nothing could be farther from the truth. Yet that is what Communism gives you— lies covered with fantasy without an ounce of truth.

My parents believed in truth, hard work, and justice, yet they found themselves living in a country where all of that was stripped away. The people began to see Fidel Castro for who he really was, and a new revolution started to brew in the hearts of my countrymen. All over the island people prepared, and plans were made for a time when Fidel Castro could be overthrown.

The Soviet Union was backing Castro, and the newly elected president of the United States, John F. Kennedy, seemed to be on our side. So many Cubans had left the country already, but they wanted to come home and get their country back. A plan was devised for the overthrow of Castro. Backed by American firepower and with help from the CIA, a group of Cuban exiles would invade Cuba and overthrow the government. So on April 17, 1961, fifteen hundred men landed in a swampy snake- and crocodile-infested area on the southern coast of Cuba known as the Bay of Pigs.

I do not know what happened or why it occurred, but at the last minute Kennedy withheld the air and naval support he promised, and Castro easily killed or captured nearly all of the invaders. I always figured Kennedy got cold feet or was convinced by the Socialist element in his own party not to go through with it. No matter the reason, it was a devastating blow to our family and my country.

Two of my cousins were in that group of fifteen hundred men. They were both captured and taken to prison. The beatings and torture they endured were heinous. We feared we would never see them again. However, Castro loved to extort money from the Cuban people, so all of my extended family pooled their money and bought their way out of prison.

All of this was very hard on me. I was in college in America, and my family was losing everything back home in my beloved country. Every letter from home brought news of more injustice. The stories of terrible atrocities were endless. Fidel promised the people he would be their savior, but instead he became their tormentor.

He was quite the chameleon. In the beginning he was so smooth talking and supportive of the common working person. After he came to power, however, he turned on them. One of the first officers to join Castro was assassinated because he spoke out against the corruption of the Communist system. The government tried to cover up his death, but word spread like wildfire through our island community.

It is such a tragic event when you watch the government come and take away everything you have worked hard to attain. Castro confiscated so many companies and family farms. It devastated our island. They took prosperous sugar cane fields and tried to turn them into rice patties. The climate was not right for this, and it caused the decimation of one of our main sources of industry.

The private school where my father worked came under scrutiny. The Castro regime did not want anything taught that went against the Communist way of life. A school teaching the merits of God and the redemption of Jesus Christ would not work well with the godless propaganda now being spouted from the public education system. Needless to say most of the teachers in the school had to flee.

My father was one of the last holdouts at the school. He really hated the thought of abandoning the area, but Castro's government was confiscating buildings and property little by little. My father was always a well-respected man in our country, so because of his knowledge and teaching ability he was a target for the Communists. They really wanted him to teach in their universities, training up a new generation in the ideals of Marxism. Because my father wanted no part of it, he soon became enemy number one.

I was a Cuban citizen living in America, but I still had the opportunity to travel home to see my family. It was so sad to see the island paradise I once loved being transformed into a wasteland of Communist failure. People who had plenty to eat before now went hungry. Where once we had local doctors helping the sick, now the government controlled our health care and people went untreated. My countrymen were dying because only the chosen received medical assistance. We were promised universal healthcare but received universal hardship instead.

Even though the country was in shambles, it was still good to be home to see my family for a short visit. My mother's cooking was a welcomed feast, and the love of my siblings warmed my heart. Part of me wanted to come home and help my family through this ordeal, but my father believed it was better for me to stay in America. Getting my degree and establishing roots there would lead to a successful future. As long as Castro and the Communists controlled Cuba, there was no hope for prosperity.

One evening before my return trip to the states, my father and I discussed the issue of my next semester of college. Because Castro allowed no money of any kind to leave the country, this made paying my tuition a serious complication. Before I could fly out of the country, all my possessions would be searched. If any money was found on me, I would be sent to jail. You see the dilemma we faced.

The Presbyterian church running my father's school put money directly into his account at the bank. We both knew if we could get his signed check out of the country, my next semester of college would be paid.

As I told you before, my father was a brilliant man. He devised a plan to get the money for my tuition out of the country. Daddy took a brand-new tube of toothpaste out of the box. Back then they were still made out of a thin piece of aluminum. At the bottom of the toothpaste it was rolled up a couple of times and sealed with a special kind of glue. Carefully he unrolled the tube at the bottom. Using a sharp knife he carefully sliced open the sealed area. Next, he folded the check and wrapped it in thin plastic then placed it back inside the tube along with the toothpaste. With the check secure he glued the opening shut and rolled it back together. Once the toothpaste was placed back in the box, you could never tell it was ever opened.

We were not sure if it would work, but it was our only option at the time. The next day I would fly back to America as long as we could successfully get past the soldiers at the airport. If the secreted money was found, it would mean incarceration for Daddy and me.

The trip to the Havana airport the next morning was nerve racking to say the least. Upon arrival we headed to the gate area where I would be checked by the armed security guards. They were more like hired thugs paid by Castro to intimidate and control the people. Men with tattered, dirty uniforms, long beards, and weapons searched every person about to board the plane.

We watched as the lady in front of us began to go through the physical interrogation. They tore open every item in her bag. There was no care or concern, just open destruction. When the soldier came to her tube of toothpaste, he picked it up, unscrewed the cap, and squeezed out every bit of it. Immediately my heart sank, as I knew they would do the same thing with mine. Fear gripped my soul at the thought of them finding the check. Not only would my father and I end up in jail, but we would never see each other again. My father reassured me God was on our side.

The time came; we were next in line. Ruthlessly the soldier began going through my things. When he came to the box of toothpaste, he carefully looked it over then tossed it aside with the rest of my things. He never opened the box. I could not believe it. After a few more moments, I was told I could pass. I hugged my father and left. God protected me; the whole incident seemed miraculous to me at the time. Like I stated in the beginning, I feel my life has been blessed.

This was not the only incident of ingenuity my father de-vised for getting money to me for my college tuition. Being a well-respected teacher in the country for years, my daddy had many friends. A couple of pilots for Cubana Airlines assisted him with getting money out of the country for me. Daddy would meet with them the day before and give it to them. They knew where they could hide it on the plane so it was not discovered.

Resistance to tyranny becomes the Christian and social duty of each individual.

— JOHN HANCOCK

My roommate at college knew all about my family situation and what was occurring back home. She was very supportive. Whenever tuition time came around she always encouraged me not to worry, reassuring me God had the situation under control.

Just before my next semester tuition came due, I received a letter from my father. When I looked inside I found only several postcards. There was nothing written on them so I was confused. The next day my father called me from Cuba to see if I received the letter. I knew he could not talk openly be-cause most calls were monitored so asking him about tuition money was difficult. Communists love to monitor your calls and listen for any reference that is negative against their form of government. It is one of the ways they maintain control and eliminate their opposition.

As soon as I told my father I received the letter, he replied, "That is so good. Ana, you need to check out those postcards; they are the last ones I can get because they are closing the school." I was confused by what he said, so I asked if he was sending anymore. He stated carefully, "Ana, you need to save them. They are the last ones I can get so check them out." It then occurred to me Daddy was trying to tell me there was a check somewhere in those postcards.

When I got off the phone, I told my roommate about the call and quickly we ran back to the room. We took each post-card out of the envelope, holding them up to the light. The last card revealed the secret. My daddy carefully fused two postcards with a check between. We were both so surprised. I turned to my roommate and said, "My daddy would have been a terrific thief." We laughed as I separated the cards and retrieved the check.

My roommate said, "Ana, even if you did not receive the check, you had nothing to fear. I told my papa about the situation, and he said he would pay your tuition if the money does not come. He loves you like you were his own daughter." Those words brought tears to my eyes. It reassured my faith that all things work together for good to them who love the Lord.

My family was going through a difficult time and as things began to get worse, they knew their only hope was to escape. For my mother and siblings, that might be simple, but for my father it would be a whole different story.

The decision to leave your home is a difficult one. All over the island people were risking their lives to leave the Communist nightmare pervading our homeland. Doctors and lawyers fled the country by the hundreds. The most educated of the popu-lace found any way they could to leave. I can only imagine the bittersweet feeling they had when they saw the flag of America flying over the rampart of the nation.

Boat upon boat carried people watching for that first glimpse of newfound freedom. They left everything behind to start over in a land where opportunity reigned supreme. Doctors and lawyers gladly waited tables in America until they were able to learn the language so they could practice their chosen professions.

Mommy and Daddy knew they would also have to sacrifice everything they owned for freedom. The home where they raised their children must be left behind. Possessions no longer matter when your family's safety is on the line.

Leaving the country had to be done discreetly. Castro and his Communist cronies did not take kindly to people leaving the island hellhole they created. So, carefully my parents began to give away their possessions. Throughout our home things slowly disappeared. Large items had to be distributed during the night when people were asleep. You could not just pull a truck up to the house in broad daylight; it would elicit way too much attention.

Each night in the community people brought their rocking chairs out onto the front porch. The family sat together and talked with the neighbors who were sitting across the street on their porches. Little traffic was in our area so the conversations were rarely interrupted. When bedtime came they just carried the chairs back into the house.

On one particular night my mother did something very different. Instead of sitting on our own porch, they carried the rockers across the street and sat on our neighbor's porch with them. The evening progressed much the same way until bedtime arrived. Their rockers, as well as my family's, were carried inside their house and my family went home. It was my mother's clever way of giving the chairs to the neighbors without raising suspicion in the community. Had Fidel known what they were doing, he would have jailed them all.

Remember Communism cannot tolerate the idea of different opinion or God-fearing people. It must crush those principles so their humanistic, atheistic propaganda can work.

The time came for my family to make their way to America, the land of the free. My mother and father knew they could not leave at the same time. Everything would have to be done with logical, careful planning.

They agreed my mother and older sister would leave the island first. Because official American recognition of the Cuban government ended, we had no US embassy to contact to get a visa to enter the country legally. So my mother and sister took a flight to Jamaica. It was not uncommon for Cubans to visit Jamaica so this did not raise the attention of the authorities.

Once in Jamaica, my mother and sister stayed there for a couple of months until they received the necessary visa to travel to America. When they arrived in Miami, Florida, a whole new life was ignited. They came with nothing—no money, no possessions, just the clothes on their backs. They had to leave everything behind, but they once again had their freedom.

Escaping the country for my father and younger sister would prove to be much more difficult. As I said before, my father was wanted by the Castro government to teach Communist principles in the university. Because he declined, they were not about to let him leave. They were determined to change his mind one way or another.

My daddy and sister had to wait about three months before they tried to leave the country. Because my mother and other sister were already gone, the awareness that my father might flee was heightened. His face was well known in the country, and Castro made sure the soldiers at the airport kept an eye out for him.

The day finally arrived for my sister and daddy to attempt their escape from the tyranny of Fidel Castro. When they arrived at the Havana airport, they split up, feeling it would help keep them from being noticed. My sister was able to easily move through the security without much attention. My father would have to be much more clandestine. If Castro's thugs saw him, he knew he would be taken captive.

Fortunately for my father he was not a very tall man, so he devised a clever idea. Because there was a large number of people in the airport, my father used the crowd to hide him. He carefully got into the center of the crowd and crouched a bit. He encouraged them to gather close so he would not be seen. Miraculously the crowd of people willfully complied.

As they neared the opening of the plane, my father spotted a young woman who was very familiar with him. She was standing at the door looking at people as they went in. He knew if she saw him it was all over. He quietly convinced the crowd of people around him to rush the opening of the plane. As they neared the opening, they quickly overwhelmed the young woman at the door, allowing my father to sneak onto the plane undiscovered by Castro's soldiers.

Before long my father and sister were on their way to Jamaica. Once they arrived they followed the same procedures my mother used a few months earlier. Within a few months they had their visas and were on their way to America. When my father and sister stepped off the plane and set their feet on the soil of freedom, our family was safe. Once again we were united. They arrived with nothing but their safety. It was enough.

★ ★ ★

Even though I loved growing up in Cuba, my home country was no longer the same. Within a few short years I became an American citizen. It did no good to send money or food to family and friends back on the island. The Communist government confiscated anything valuable. The only hope anyone had was to escape to America.

Ever since I was a young girl, my father instilled the principle of hard work in me. He always said, "Ana, if you work hard you will be compensated." In America, it was not long before I found that to be the case. In fact, my entire family became profitable in their chosen endeavors.

I now proudly sing the song, "God, Bless America," for it is truly the land I love. My former home country of Cuba is no longer the same. Years of Communism destroyed the place I once proudly called home.

Many of the people now in Cuba have no initiative; they do not care. They have become beaten down by the system. There is no opportunity to get ahead or for advancement. You are paid the same wage whether you do a good job or not. The incentive to work hard is no longer there. Marxism has destroyed the people and their morality. Where there was once a land of people who faithfully worked hard, helped their neighbors, and worshipped God, it was replaced with immorality, laziness, and humanism.

Some of the people who have grown up under Castro have learned to be totally dependent on the government for everything. Why work hard to get ahead when the government will take from those who do and give it to those who won't? It truly is a sad state of affairs.

Unfortunately, most do not know any better for this is the only way of life they have ever known. In fact, when the little ones now come to America, they believe the government should give them everything. Sadly, some people here also believe the same thing.

Even though we left everything behind to come to America, I am extremely thankful. This was never more appreciated than a short time ago. Most of my family lives near Miami, Florida, around the area known as Little Havana. About a week before I came to visit, a serious incident occurred with my niece and her husband.

One evening while he was in the kitchen washing his hands, he collapsed to the floor. My niece heard the commotion and rushed into the room where she found him. When she checked his pulse, she found nothing, so immediately she began to pray while starting CPR. She quickly yelled for her daughter to call 911.

He was dead; there was no use in continuing to administer CPR. But she did and she prayed, pouring out her heart to God. She did not remember how long it took for the paramedics to arrive, but once they got on the scene they took over the life-saving procedures.

Things looked very bad for some time until miraculously they were able to revive him. They transported him to a nearby hospital where they scheduled him for a heart catheterization. After a few moments they found the blockage, and thanks to modern-day medicine they repaired the problem. By the time I arrived you never would have known he had a problem.

As I sat there with my niece, I began to thank God we were in America. Had my niece and her husband been in Cuba, he would be dead. They were certainly not some of the privileged few who would have received care or treatment. His life would not have been any value to the Communist government.

★ ★ ★

When 102 English pilgrims boarded the Mayflower, they left behind the only home they ever knew. They came to a land in search of freedom, a place to enjoy the blessings of God. Even though they endured great hardship, we can certainly look back now and say it was well worth it.

Looking back through my life, I can most certainly say the same thing. We endured trouble, lost everything we owned, but in the end the United States truly became our haven of rest. For my family, America has become the land of opportunity, the dwelling of liberty, and a nation God has truly

blessed!

"Blessed is the nation
whose God is the LORD."
— PSALM 33:12

WERE SO
Gallantly
Streaming

With the pilot and co-pilot rendered unable to fly, the responsibility fell to me. There was only one problem: I had never piloted any type of aircraft in my life. Harvard and Yale may be some of America's top educational institutions, but no Ivy League school could compete with the immediate education I received eighteen hundred feet in the air and nine thousand miles away from home.

My name is Mackey. This is my story of America.

★ ★ ★

They say what doesn't kill you makes you stronger. I definitely agree with that statement wholeheartedly. Not only does it make you stronger, it makes you smarter. Survival is an education process where the final exam means more than just a passing grade. Fail its test and you never get another.

My life's education began when I graduated from a small high school in West Virginia. For me there was no thought of college. I went to the neighboring state of Virginia and got a job doing road construction. I was not afraid of hard work; I was raised to make a living by the sweat of your brow. If a man doesn't work, neither should he eat—that's the rule of where I grew up.

My life on the road crew did not last long because Uncle Sam decided I needed a new type of schooling. Still wet behind the ears with no real life experience, I was drafted by the army to serve my country. My classroom of life began when I was sent to Fort Knox, Kentucky, for basic training. After my graduation they sent me to Fort Eustis, Virginia, for advanced individual training then onto Fort Bragg, North Carolina, where I became part of the 187th Assault Helicopter Company.

Over the next eight weeks I was trained on everything it takes to maintain an assault helicopter. I was responsible for it all. The amount of information presented to me was overwhelming. I learned so much so fast I could barely keep up. My training landed me a position of crew chief, and it was my job to maintain these flying gunships. If anything went wrong, it would be my responsibility to fix it.

The army truly believes in cross-utilization. In fact I believe they probably invented the term multitasking. Not only had they trained me to keep this bird in the air, they also taught me how to fire an M60 machine gun out of the open door of a chopper, restrained only by a simple lap belt. They believe in maximizing your potential.

Manning the M60 machine gun on a helicopter was not a popular job because of the exposed position in the air and the legend that a door gunner on a Huey gunship had the average life span of five minutes. Of course this was exaggerated, but the point was certainly made. My new career path would be very dangerous, one I might not survive.

My eight weeks of schooling went quickly, and before I knew it I was gallantly streaming across the sky headed for my first assignment: Vietnam.

When we arrived at Bien Hoa Air Base, I did not think it was so bad. We had asphalt, barracks, and places to go, so what was the big deal? This wasn't the jungle warfare I heard about. I was soon in for a rude awakening, however, because this is not where I stayed.

I still remember my first night in the country. I, like most of the other guys, lay there totally scared to death. The sound of bombs going off was all I heard. Each detonation brought goose bumps to my skin and a lump to my throat. On more than one occasion that night I crawled under my bed, I was so terrified. I felt like a coward and a fool until I realized I was not the only one hiding.

Finally to my relief the commander came and told us the bombs were outgoing. There was nothing for us to worry about. I felt foolish, for all this time I just knew we were under attack. I was never in any danger at all—well, not yet anyway. Boy, was I ever in for an education.

The next morning we boarded a C-130 airplane and were flown to Tay Ninh. Our job would be to support the 25th Infantry Division. Talk about a difference! You certainly could not compare Bien Hoa with Tay Ninh. We arrived in a place little more than a giant mudhole and no asphalt runway. In fact, the army had to take a heavy-grade medal gridding with waves in it and link them together to form an area where a plane could land.

When the plane slammed onto this rough surface, it felt like hitting a series of speed bumps going ninety mph in an old jalopy. There was nothing smooth about it, but the pilot got us on the ground. We no sooner got off the plane when we were handed shovels and some sandbags and told to start digging.

And dig we did. It seemed like all I did was dig ditches and fill sandbags, but it was necessary; when the monsoons came, we needed them for protection. We had to lay down wooden pallets on which to pitch our tents. We would then take sandbags and use them for drainage to keep out the water. There were fifteen to twenty of us assigned to one tent.

I don't remember how long I was there until they flew me back to Bien Hoa Air Base for a two-week in-country training. I was trained in the states, but this one was different. Before you could go on any combat missions, you had to have this training. Up until then the only thing I could go on was a mail or supply run—basically just anything safe. The only way I could go on an assault would be if I volunteered.

After the first week I grew bored with the training. I had only a few days left when I turned to my friend John and said, "You know after formation we have nothing left to do today. We have nowhere to go and no one to report to; we are going to spend the day lollygagging around. I am getting so bored, and this is nothing but a bunch of crap."

John replied, "Well let's go talk to the platoon sergeant."

We walked into the camp and told the sergeant we wanted something to do. Flabbergasted, he replied, "Boys, we are flying all combat support missions right now. I can't use you.

Mackey, I know you have a lot of air time, but that is all in the states." John and I already decided we were not going to take no for an answer, so we pressed the issue. The sergeant said, "OK, I have a combat mission going out tomorrow, and the crew chief and gunner need a break. You have to volunteer for the mission before I can let you go."

I looked at John and he looked at me, and together we volunteered for the mission. Boy, was that ever a mistake!

On July 2, 1967, John and I boarded a D-model Huey, which they called a "slick." It was used to haul troops and re-supplies to our combat areas. The excitement I felt was only matched by my anxiety. This was my first air assault combat mission. My life's education was now about to hit the graduate school level.

We sat there waiting for our pilot to arrive. It wasn't long before we saw this guy strutting across the runway. He was shaved, spit shined, and cut to fit. He looked as if he just stepped out of a catalog. John and I on the other hand looked a mess. We had not shaved in three days, and we were wearing muddy T-shirts.

The pilot had been in the country for only eleven days, so I greeted him by saying, "This is your lucky day."

He looked at my shirt and said, "Mackey, I have heard some bad reports on you. I don't know if I want to fly with you or not."

I asked, "What do you mean, sir?"

He replied, "Well I have heard some stuff about you."

Nonchalantly I replied, "Well they sent us over here to do a job; we go where the action is. Don't worry, we will make sure you get broke in just right." Now let me remind you, we had never been on an air assault combat mission, but he did not know that. I figured if he knew this was our first he would keep us from going, and we wanted to do something exciting for a change.

John's role for the day was crew chief, while I manned the M60 machine gun. I stepped inside the helicopter and strapped myself in behind the pilot. John was directly to my right, and we were both ready for action. Well at least we naively thought we were.

As we lifted off we veered right and headed about three miles south of the Saigon River. We were one of ten gunships making up this mission. In an instant we went from calm to extreme fighting. Rounds poured out the front of my M60 as I hung out the open door of our chopper. John shouted instructions as we started taking heavy fire.

Soon I heard the sound of armor-piercing bullets penetrating the cabin of our Huey. This was no game; this was real. We volunteered ourselves right into the middle of a war zone, and I began to wonder if I would make it out alive.

My mind focused on the fact that just days earlier I was sitting in classes and learning about war, and now I was actually fighting it. I was quickly snapped back to the present when I heard screams coming from the cockpit.

An armor-piercing round entered at the base of the right side of the gunship. It traveled through both legs of the co-pilot, across the console, and through the leg of the pilot where it severed an artery. We began to spin uncontrollably as we dropped quickly out of the sky.

The co-pilot cried out in excruciating pain, "We have been hit. I've been shot, I've been shot!" as the Huey slammed into the ground below. Throughout the entire incident I fired my gun, but now a new course of action was required. John and I both stowed our weapons and moved into action.

On the side of the pilot and co-pilot seats were quick-release mechanisms. We grabbed them, sprung the release, and pulled the seats back. The pilot was screaming in agony as we pulled him out of the chair. Without thinking and just by pure instinct, I crawled into the cockpit and sat as the pilot. With no hesitation John shoved the seat forward, and I was ready to fly this ship out of there. Only one problem remained: I had never flown anything in my life.

To move to the pilot seat, I had to disconnect my helmet from the communication system. This is how we communicated with each other as well as with other gunships in the area. I was so scared at the time I forgot to hook myself back up once I got into the pilot seat. I was a man with no flight experience, but I was about to get a crash course in Huey 101.

I began jerking and pulling on things, trying to get this bird back in the air. We were under heavy fire, and the co-pilot was trying to give me instructions all the while his left leg was squirting blood like a pump. It just shot out of each side relentlessly.

We had a short distance to go to be able to get over the trees, and I started screaming, "We are not going to make it!" The basic fundamentals of flying this beast I knew. I had been in and around these gunships long enough to become familiar with how they worked. Yet it was a different feeling sitting in the seat trying to fly it. I knew I needed all the help I could get so I kept calling out, "I need help! We are not going to make it, we are not going to make it." No reply came. I could not figure out why no one was answering me until John realized

I was not hooked to the communication system. He grabbed the cord, plugged me back in, and immediately I began to hear some reassuring words.

Under heavy attack I managed to get the Huey off the ground, then I headed toward the tops of the trees. We just barely cleared them as the skids on the chopper clipped the tops, but no matter, we were on our way out. As we started gaining altitude, I heard my captain call out on the radio. He was in the chopper right behind me, and they were making their way up to our side.

The co-pilot's head was slumping forward as blood continued to pour out of his leg. I looked over to the captain in the other chopper and said, "This is Mackey. I am flying this helicopter, and basically I don't know what I am doing. The co-pilot has been talking to me, but he is not totally coherent. I need him alive to help me fly this bird, or we will all be dead."

The captain radioed back saying we should head to Cu Chi; it was the closest place to get to a medevac. We were thirty minutes away, and without stopping the bleeding I knew the co-pilot would never survive.

Here I was on my first combat mission—pilot in the back being worked on by John, co-pilot in the front losing blood, and me flying a helicopter for the first time. I was certainly getting an education the hard way. The co-pilot told me, "You have got to do something about this bleeding." I looked at him as if he was crazy. How was I supposed to stop his bleeding and fly this bird at the same time?

The co-pilot was still functioning well enough to give me some instructions. He told me, "Take the knob on the stick and lock the collective down, then reach over here and stop this bleeding." I looked at him and replied, "You are going to have to hold on because I can't get this thing on the ground. We are eighteen hundred feet in the air and I will kill us all." He said, "I am not asking you to get us down; I am saying you have to reach over here and stop this blood."

Taking a firm grasp on the controls with my left hand, I reached over and slid my right hand palm up under the co-pilot's leg. Straining my arm and shoulder, I rotated my hand a bit counterclockwise so I could stick my thumb into the entry wound on the inside of his thigh and my index finger into the exit wound on the outside. I wasn't sure if it would work, but it greatly slowed his blood loss.

There I was flying a helicopter for the first time with one hand on the controls and the other stuck into the leg of my co-pilot—not exactly what I expected when I volunteered for this mission.

As we got closer to Cu Chi, the co-pilot was getting worse. Captain Wagoner in the chopper beside me called the tower and told them to clear the runway. He warned them about what was going on. As I neared Cu Chi I could see the runway on the right side of the compound, and up ahead of it was the hospital with a helipad built right inside the courtyard. I had no intention of aiming for the runway; I was headed straight for the hospital.

As I bypassed the runway, the captain began to scream at me, "Where the hell are you going?" I replied, "I am going to the hospital." That was the last I had to say about it; going directly to the hospital made the most sense to me.

When I started my approach, the co-pilot's neck went limp and I got frightened. I flew this far; I would now have to land this thing and I didn't have a clue in the world how to do it. So I did the only thing I could; I reached over and started banging on the co-pilot to get his attention. I managed to get him coherent enough to tell me what pedals to push. He said, "Make sure your RPMs do not get too low, or we will fall out of the sky and crash." *Great, some more encouraging words—just want I needed.*

I started yelling on the intercom, which also transmitted to Captain Wagoner, "We are not going to make it. I am too steep."

He replied, "Just hold where you got it. You are all right." So by the grace of him, the co-pilot, and most certainly God, I managed to put the Huey on the ground.

I had no clue how to shut it off, but that did not matter, I immediately jumped out and grabbed the pilot, throwing him on the stretcher they had waiting for us. I then pulled the co-pilot out and carried him around the chopper so I could put him on the other one. They were quickly whisked away to surgery, and Captain Wagoner came over to shut down the gunship.

All in all it was a memorable first mission. I prayed to God they would not all be like this. I was bored and wanted action, but this was certainly more than I expected.

Walking around the helicopter, I counted thirty-two bullet holes. It is a wonder we even got off the ground, let alone made it back. A maintenance pilot came and moved the chopper to a service area where we could further assess the damage. Before this unit would be allowed to fly again, it had to be thoroughly checked. I could tell by looking, it would take more than duct tape to fix this bird. (Yes it's true; we often used duct tape to patch holes in those helicopters. It really can fix anything.)

A Huey helicopter has almost all of its innermost mechanics in the belly of the unit. It is about a foot deep and runs all the way from the front to the back rotors. Because it was my job to ensure this bird could get back in the sky, I was assigned to go through it with a fine-tooth comb.

I began by pulling the floor out of the cabin of the chopper. The bell crank, which operates the push/pull tubes that control the rotor, is normally about an inch to an inch and a quarter; however, there was only about a quarter inch left because a round went through it. I have no clue what held it together. We really should have fallen out of the sky.

We went to work repairing all the mechanical failures, and before long we had it flyable. Another pilot was sent in so John and I could be flown back to our station at Tay Ninh.

I climbed into the gunner's seat, and John sat in the seat to my right; one pilot was in front of us. He radioed the tower to get permission to take off then turned to me and said, "Get up here." I just sat there and said nothing. The pilot called out, "Mackey, get up here." I said, "Get up where?" He sternly replied, "Get up here in this co-pilot seat." I said, "The hell with you; I am not getting up there in that seat. No disrespect to you and your rank, but I am not getting up there." He said, "Yes you are. I am giving you a direct order. Now get yourself up here."

What else could I do? I crawled into the front seat and stepped in a pool of blood about two inches deep. It had formed into a substance like gelatin all over the cabin floor. The pilot turned to me and said, "OK, let's go. Fly us out of here."

I looked at him and replied, "You are out of your ever-loving mind. Do you want to die or what? I am shaking so bad there is no way I can do this."

From the time I landed at the hospital until now I smoked two packs of cigarettes and I didn't even smoke. There was no way I was going to do it.

The pilot took the controls, getting us about twenty feet off the ground. He turned to me, taking his hands off the controls, and said, "OK, it is all yours."

I grabbed the stick and said, "Are you crazy? You do want to die." But we didn't die; I managed to fly us across country without incident.

As we neared the airfield, the pilot called in and told them what was going on. We were going to make our approach. When we got to about thirty or forty feet from the ground, I could not get us down. I was so stressed out at this point I kept going back or forward. Then I started going from side to side but could not get down.

The maintenance major on the ground was standing there looking up at my troubles. I just could not get us on the ground. I looked over at the pilot and said, "You are going to have to take over because I cannot get us on the ground. I am going to tear this thing up." I just let go of the controls so he grabbed them. Within seconds we landed.

Major Burns walked over to the chopper and yelled, "Who in the hell is flying my helicopter?" With a wide smile, the pilot pointed to me. I was busy looking for a place to hide. My career as a pilot was over before it ever really began. I certainly received an education I never forgot. I still could not believe all this happened on my first combat mission. Mental note to self, *Never volunteer again.*

Two weeks passed after my great adventure in the skies. I was sent into Cu Chi for an assignment. The pilot who was shot on my first combat mission was sent stateside for surgery and recuperation. The co-pilot had both of his legs opened up, and they were letting them heal from the inside out. I never knew what happened to him, but the pilot and I would meet again.

The maintenance major came out and told me I was to report to Bien Hoa for a news conference about the incident near Saigon. I looked at him and said, "No way. I have been writing home to my mother just complaining about the weather and food. I told her I only made milk runs delivering supplies; she has no clue what happened. There is no way I am doing the news conference."

He stated, "Yes you are."

I replied, "No I am not." Moments later he left and I felt I won the battle.

Thirty minutes passed, and the company commander returned instead. He motioned for me to get in the jeep with him. I told him, "Sir, I am not going."

He looked at me sternly and said, "Yes you are. You are going into the orderly room and write a letter. We will ship it out of here, and then you are going to that news conference." I knew I had no choice. I did not want to go because I do not like being in front of a large crowd, and more importantly I did not want my mother to know I lied about the danger I was in.

When we arrived in Bien Hoa, I walked into the conference area, and there must have been about sixty reporters staring back at me. So many large microphones were standing in front of me you would have thought the president was showing up. My knees were knocking so hard I was wondering if I would even be able to stand.

The commander told me, "Just tell the story like it happened, but don't use any other names. They know your name, but don't mention any others because the pilot and co-pilot were wounded. Their families may not know anything about it yet."

> *The time is near at hand which must determine whether Americans are to be free men or slaves.*
>
> — GEORGE WASHINGTON

I stepped behind the microphones, and while stuttering I told them about the incident. I managed to mumble my way through it for the most part. When I finished one reporter in the back room stood up and said, "Well, now that we know you can fly this helicopter and Uncle Sam knows you can fly this helicopter, what does the future represent for you? Are you going to flight school or warrant officer school?"

I looked straight back at him and replied, "I have a short period of time left to go here, and to do what you are suggesting I will have to re-enlist. So the answer is no; as soon as my time is finished, I am heading back to West by God Virginia." That ended the news conference rather quickly.

For the next several months things were interesting. My days consisted of maintaining choppers and combat assault missions as a gunner or crew chief. I was in several helicopters that were shot down by the Vietcong, but I always managed to avoid being hit by any enemy fire.

War in Vietnam was so political. We would fight for weeks to take a hill. Then we would hold it for two or three months until we were told to leave the area. As soon as we left, the North Vietnamese would come in and take it back. The South

Vietnamese really had no way to defend themselves. They were mostly farmers trying to scratch out an existence from the ground. This is where I learned how the Communists preyed upon the weak. They either forced them to do what they wanted or coerced them to follow their ways.

We could only fire on the enemy if they fired on us first. Unfortunately, we sometimes didn't know who the enemy was. We helped a village fight the Vietcong, and the villagers became our friends. Days later we returned to find a woman with a child and a ten-year-old girl firing rifles at us because the North Vietnamese forced them to. It was a miserable period of life for all involved. Some images we can never wash from our minds; they just sit there on the back burner.

The Vietcong placed hand grenades under the arms of little children and sent them up to an American soldier. When they picked up the smiling little child, the grenade fell and killed both. The North Vietnamese had no respect for human life—not for their own children or for anyone else. They even skinned innocent villagers alive and hanged them from a tree if they did not fight with them.

We flew into some tough areas picking up bodies of dead soldiers. Some were there for twelve or more hours. It was a miserable assignment loading their blue, bloated bodies into the chopper. I watched as men I loved like brothers died and then had to pull them out of a war zone. It was gut wrenching.

On one particular mission I picked up seven dead soldiers in our helicopter. We only had an area of about four feet inside the cabin, so all I could do was stack their lifeless bodies on top of one another. I meant no disrespect, but it was the only way I could get them out of there.

Far too often I had to pick up limbs and body parts of soldiers so I could try to match them with their owners. It was an impossible task. I am sure there were some people who went home in body bags with different limbs than they brought to Vietnam.

The South Vietnamese soldiers were not always a courageous bunch. On more than one occasion I had to throw them on a transport to take them into an area where we were facing combat. We flew in with our troops and theirs. If we started receiving fire, it was radioed back that we needed support. When a South Vietnamese soldier heard this, they didn't want to go in. They were all for you going in and them backing you up, but they did not want to take the lead in fighting for their own freedom.

Liberty does not come cheap; standing for what is right during a war or in your own hometown always takes courage. Notice, I did not say for what you believe in. Many people are willing to fight for what they believe in, but it does not make it right. The Vietcong fought for what they believed, but their godless, Communist way of life was certainly the wrong way of thinking.

About three months after our adventure, the pilot shot in our first mission returned from the states. He had been patched up successfully, and now he was cleared to fly again. He was reunited with John and me as we prepared for another mission.

The fateful day the pilot was shot and I took over flying was a series of firsts. It was the first combat flying mission for the pilot, and it was the first combat assault mission for John and me. This time the assignment was much more benign. We were going to be transporting supplies. I thought, *Well at least we should not have any trouble on this mission.* Boy, was I wrong, for Murphy's Law would rear its ugly head yet again.

I was the crew chief on this mission, and it was my responsibility to ensure the load was properly balanced so the helicopter could safely get off the ground. Usually this was not an issue because the pilot trusted the crew chief to do his job, but on this occasion things did not work out that way.

John and I were loading the chopper when I noticed it was unbalanced. I told the crew not to put anything else on because it could not handle it. Yet the pilot ignored my warnings and kept piling footlockers and supplies on. The items were not stacked properly, and too much of a load was past the center of gravity. There was no way we could get off the ground.

I looked at the pilot and said, "This is not going to work; we can't get off the ground. We have too much weight on it past the center of gravity."

He looked at me arrogantly and said, "We will make it."

A six-foot-tall fence with concertina wire along the top enclosed the area. As we climbed in the chopper, the pilot fired up the unit and began to do a hover check. The machine had a lot of hours on it with several bullet holes patched with duct tape.

When he rose off the ground, the machine bled off and went back down. He decided to try again. On the second attempt the same thing happened. He turned to the co-pilot and said, "I am going to fire it up and head over there toward that fence."

This had gone on long enough, and I figured it was time for me to do something so I yelled, "I am strictly against this. This is my responsibility; I am loadmaster on this helicopter.

If I feel you are not doing it right, I have the authority to tell you it is not correct. I am going to put this in the logbook that I am against us trying to fly with this load. It is too heavy, and too much of it is sitting past the center of gravity." However, it did not matter because he pulled rank on me and said, "Well, we are going. I don't care what you say because I know what I am doing. I am the pilot and I know more."

So the pilot increased the power and off we went . . . for only fifty yards, though, when the skids hit the ground. We bounced in the air and went another fifty yards then back down as the skids slammed into the ground again. Determined to prove he was right, he increased the power and up we went then right down into the middle of that fence. The sound of a helicopter being torn in half filled the air as one of the medal posts on the fence went through the tail of our chopper.

Officers scattered everywhere as people ran for cover. The helicopter was ruined. The transmission was destroyed, and the tail rotor was torn off. John and I just sat there for a moment shaking our heads.

Someone called the company commander. When the major arrived he walked over and looked at the stuck helicopter and asked, "Where is the crew chief?" I was on the other side of the chopper fuming because of the incident, so when I walked over to the major, he said, "I need to talk to you."

We walked a few feet away so he could get me by myself and he asked, "What in the hell is going on?" I told him, "Well sir, she had too much weight on her. We've had this unit here for a while now. It has a lot of hours on it, and every time they tried to get it in the air it would bleed off."

The major asked, "Did the pilot pull a hover check?" I said, "Yes sir, he did." Frustrated, the major questioned, "Did you write in the logbook that the load was too heavy for this trip?" I smiled and stated, "Yes sir, I most certainly did."

Now the major was furious and screamed, "You mean to tell me you told the pilot this helicopter could not fly out of here and he did not listen?"

I confidently said, "Yes sir, you are correct." He nodded and said, "OK, you can go." I watched as the major headed back to the helicopter. As soon as he got up to the pilot, he said, "I hope you have a damn big checkbook because you are going to be paying for that helicopter."

Life taught me another great lesson. A prideful arrogant spirit leads to a fall. We all had important jobs to do. It did not matter if your rank was higher or not. You had to listen to people with different skill sets than you. No one can know everything. When you are a part of a team, everyone is important; everyone has value. I guess the pilot forgot that lesson. I am glad I never did.

My time in Vietnam was coming to a conclusion. At the thirty-day mark they basically shut you down. It means you no longer go on any assaults or combat missions unless you volunteer. We were losing guys left and right so we were shorthanded. I decided to go to the company commander and volunteer for flight duty because we were low on men. I guess I had not (quite) learned that lesson about volunteering after all. (Actually I am only jesting about volunteering. Throughout my life it has made me a better person. Besides, my country, company, and brothers in arms needed my help, so I was ready to serve.)

About six days before I was due to leave the country, I went on an air combat assault. We were to take some troops into a hostile region. Once again John and I hit the air together. He took his place as crew chief, and I strapped into the gunner position. At my feet lay 350 rounds of ammunition for my M60 machine gun. The pilot and co-pilot fired up the chopper, and soon we were in the air headed for war.

We were not in the air long before we came under heavy fire. This was a hot spot of action, and I started firing my M60 into the jungle below. The feel of the weapon recoiling into my arms after every shot seemed to get more difficult as I fired round after round. The ammunition lay linked on the cabin floor of the helicopter between my feet, and with every shot the coil of bullets got smaller.

The pilot managed to get us on the ground, and the troops filed out into the heat of combat. Within seconds we were back in the air, and John was grabbing at my shoulder.

He said, "Mackey, are you OK?"

I looked at him and replied, "Yeah sure, why do you ask?"

Puzzled, he looked and said, "Well, I thought you had been shot. I mean you never fired a single bullet when we were going in even though the chopper was hit six times. I figured you must have been shot, dead, or severely hurt." I looked at him like he was crazy and said, "John, I fired every shot. Just look. There are no bullets at my—"

My words stopped as I noticed the full string of ammunition still coiled on the floor of the helicopter. I had not fired a single shot; I had imagined everything. I knew right then I had to get off this gunship. I could have gotten all of us killed because my mind shut down.

When we got back to base, I was sent to the commander's office. He heard what happened. When I walked in he said to me, "Mackey, I should never have let you go on the mission. I should have shut you down at your thirty-day mark. With only six days to go, your mind was so afraid of dying it just checked out on you."

He was right. Fear is an interesting thing. On one occasion it propelled me to do something I had never done, then on this occasion it almost got me killed. The stress and strain we were under had almost caused me to crack. War was twenty-four hours a day, seven days a week, and many times I got only one or two hours of sleep a day.

The time finally came for me to return home. I can remember being at the Bien Hoa airfield for three hours watching the skies for my ride back to the United States. Everyone was so wired up because they knew we were heading home. The anticipation filling the air was electric.

When the plane hit the ground, we all let out a cheer. I could not wait to get on board and find a seat. So after waiting three hours, they lined us up and put us on the plane. Four stewardesses were on board, and to me every one of them was a beauty queen.

We were only on the plane fifteen minutes when they told us we had to get off. The plane had a flat tire. So off we went to wait for them to fix it. After it was repaired we headed back on until another announcement came telling us to exit once again. This time we had to get off because they forgot to fuel it up. I was beginning to think I would never get out of there.

Finally, when everything was good to go, we left Vietnam and headed for home. I can still remember landing in Hawaii. It was absolutely beautiful. The color of the water was mesmerizing. It was such a sight to behold. The different shades of it seemed to paint a picture saying, "Welcome home, Soldier."

From Hawaii I headed to California for a few days then back home to Almost Heaven West Virginia. Those words seemed truer than ever before in my life.

I was asked, "What is the most important thing you learned from your service in Vietnam?" That is a very simple question to answer. In war, when you leave your country and go to a foreign land, you know you are going to fight the enemy. In fact, when you join the armed forces, you go in with the knowledge you may at some point go to war.

I have often heard the statement, "They died fighting for their country," and it is a true statement up to a certain point. In actuality, we really die for one another.

When I went to Vietnam I was a young man from West Virginia drafted to serve his country. I believe we had more men taken per capita to Vietnam than any other state. I met many men from different parts of America who were there for the same reason I was; they were drafted.

Different races, different social status, and varying demographics really make no difference when you are sleeping in a monsoon in the jungle. You eat with them, sleep with them, and dig ditches by their sides. You develop a bond and friendship that transcends any physical differences you may have noticed before.

It no longer matters if you are rich or poor, black or white. What matters is you are willing to give everything you have to protect your fellow soldier. You have his back, and he has yours. The fight for survival outranks your differences. We were no longer Baptists, Methodists, Catholics, Presbyterians, or atheists; we were all one unit trusting in the grace of God to keep us safe.

I believe somewhere in the Bible it says something like, "No greater love than this that a man would lay down his life for his friends." Well that is what I learned in Vietnam. Every one of us came with our differences, our prejudices, and our varying ways of life. Yet during it all we learned to love one another as we loved ourselves. We put aside our individual wants and desires to protect our fellow man. No soldier left behind.

In school we learned about the Declaration of Independence and the ratification of the United States Constitution. Men from all walks of life from different states came together for a common purpose: the pursuit of liberty. They sacrificed their lives, their fortunes, and their sacred honor to establish a nation founded on the principle that all men are created equal.

On the fateful day they ratified our Constitution, they were no longer individual colonies; they became the United States of America. They came together, looked past their differences, their rampant self-interests, and formed, "One nation under God."

My heroes are all those men who gave their lives in Vietnam. They paid the ultimate sacrifice for someone else's freedom. Those of us who made it back were never the same. We came to Southeast Asia as strangers but left there as brothers.

We went to Vietnam as West Virginians, Texans, and New Yorkers, but we returned as

Americans!

WHAT IS
Your Story?

The British soldiers fired shots relentlessly, knocking the eighty-one-year-old patriot from his horse. Desperately trying to stand, he felt the brunt of a musket across his back and then into his head. Kicked, spat upon, and left for dead, this seasoned citizen managed to crawl to safety. A kind soul tended his wounds, and over the course of a month the man was nursed back to health. For ten more years the old gentleman would continue to fight for the cause of freedom. His determination and perseverance inspired a generation for liberty.

That is his story of America. What is yours?

The account you just read is completely true, yet the name of the individual is not important because you most likely don't know who he is anyway. He was an average person fighting for truth, justice, and the American way.

This is what makes our country who it is. Ordinary men and women willing to stand up for what is right—determined to help their fellow man and keep alive the ideals of our founding documents.

Politicians, celebrities, and sports heroes dot the landscape of our daily media consumption, but they do not really define who we are. The truth of America is found in our small towns and inner cities, our suburbs and backwoods. Ordinary people doing their best to love their neighbor as they love themselves. Those men and women who choose service over selfish ambitions.

Throughout our country there are people following the ideals set forth by our Founding Fathers. The ideals formed under the macro truth that all men are created equal. Many choose to look past the differences and find the common bond linking us all. We are Americans, all created in the image of God. Our Declaration of Independence ends with the words, "And for the support of this declaration, with a firm reliance on the protection of Divine Providence, we mutually pledge to each other our lives, our fortunes, and our sacred honor."

Those fifty-six signers decided they wanted to be independent from England and the king but pledged their dependence on God and one another. We need another dose of that medicine of dependence in America today.

The stories you have read in this book are true. The people in this book are average Americans just like you and me. Outside their inner circle most would never know their names, yet they have kept alive the American dream. They believe in life and liberty, faith and freedom, as well as peace and prosperity. They get up each day, love their families, their fellow man, and the God who created them. Their desire for liberty echoes throughout this great land.

I am sure you noticed how each chapter title was a portion of our national anthem. The following chapters will complete the first stanza of the "Star-Spangled Banner." The next eight stories are yet to be written, but the people who will share them are already out there waiting to be found. You may be sitting there right now reading this book and know the next story of America. This is how all the tales came to me, by word of mouth.

America must have men and women who are dedicated to keeping her free. Without the average citizen doing his or her part, we will no longer be the land of the free or the home of the brave. We will be just another country traveling down the road and falling into the failures of Socialism.

When Nathan Hale at twenty-one years of age gave his life for a country not yet founded, he spoke these final words: "I only regret that I have but one life to lose for my country." His sacrifice inspired a young nation to fight on for the cause of liberty.

I would like to leave you with the words of Noah Webster, one of our Founding Fathers and the man who gave us the first American dictionary:

> Never, my fellow citizens, let us exchange our civil and religious institutions for the wild theories of crazy projectors—or the sober, industrious, moral habits of our country for experiments in atheism and lawless democracy. Experience is a safe pilot; but experiment is a dangerous ocean, full of rocks and shoals.
>
> Our fathers were men—they were heroes and patriots—they conquered—and they bequeathed to us a rich inheritance of liberty and empire which

we have no right to surrender. We have an excellent system of religion and of government—we have wives and children and sisters to defend; and God forbid that the soil of America should sustain the wretch who lacks the will or the spirit to defend them.

Let us then rally round the independence and Constitution of our country, resolved to a man that we will never lose by folly, disunion, or cowardice what has been planned by wisdom and purchased with blood.

While the storm clouds gather far across the sea,
Let us swear allegiance to a land that's free,
Let us all be grateful for a land so fair,
As we raise our voices in a solemn prayer.
God bless America,
Land that I love.
Stand beside her, and guide her
Through the night with a light from above.
From the mountains, to the prairies,
To the oceans, white with foam
God bless America, My home sweet home
God bless America, My home sweet HOME!

— IRVING BERLIN

If you have a story you feel would be great for the next book, please visit MyStoryofAmerica.com and tell us about it.

About the Author

Dr. Michael T. George grew up in a small town in West Virginia. His father is a decorated veteran of the Vietnam War, and his service for the country instilled a sense of patriotism in Michael at a young age. That love for America took a new turn after the events of 9/11 when Michael began traveling the country sharing the inspiring stories of America to keep alive the principled ideals of our Founding Fathers.

His motivational and inspirational speaking career spans more than ten years, and he specializes in helping people become better leaders by retelling the stories that form the foundation of America. Michael is on the Board of Directors of Freedom Congress, holds a doctorate in theology from Andersonville Theological Seminary, and is a nationally sought out speaker.

For more information check out PatriotHistory.org.